THE POINT
OF LOW POINTS

A STUDY OF THE LIFE OF JOSEPH

THE POINT
OF LOW POINTS

A STUDY OF THE LIFE OF JOSEPH
KEN GURLEY

WORD AFLAME PRESS
HAZELWOOD, MO

The Point of Low Points

by Ken Gurley

Cover Design by T'Neil Walea

Published by Word Aflame Press, 8855 Dunn Road, Hazelwood, MO 63042. Printed in the United States of America.

All Scripture quotations in this book are from the King James Version of the Bible unless otherwise identified.

Composition/Song Title: IT WON'T RAIN ALWAYS
Writer Credits: Charles Aaron Wilburn / Gloria Gaither / William Gaither
Copyright: © 1981 Universal Music - Brentwood Benson Publishing (ASCAP) / William J. Gaither Music.
All rights reserved. Used by permission.

Library of Congress Cataloging-in-Publication Data

Gurley, Ken, 1957-

  The point of low points : a study of the life of Joseph / by Ken Gurley.

    pages cm

  Includes bibliographical references and index.

  ISBN 978-0-7577-4490-7 (alk. paper)

  1. Joseph, Son of Jacob. I. Title.

  BS580.J6G87 2013

  222'.11092--dc23

                              2013025423

TABLE OF CONTENTS

AUTHOR'S PREFACE

"Who wants to hear a message about low points?"

That's what I asked myself for weeks on end. I had convinced myself that the discussion of low points was a "bummer" of a subject and, to my way of thinking, was pointless.

Then came the fateful Sunday when the proverbial well ran dry. I simply had nothing I could lay my hands on to say with any degree of confidence that the Spirit was in it until I heard His gentle voice ask, "Why not talk about where you've been?" This gentle question prompted a rush of mixed emotions: hurt, sorrow, anxiety, and, curiously, hope. For where I had been was a place I could wish on no other; but what I had learned probably needed to be shared.

In my own valley experience, I pored over the story of Joseph. I studied him, his circumstances, and his reactions. So, that Sunday, I shared what I felt to be the shallowest of the low points in Joseph's life—an experience he had in Shechem. When I finished, I momentarily thought, "There, that does it. I'll never have to do that again." The Spirit, however, had other ideas.

Over the next few weeks, I continued to address this subject to profound results. For me, it was as if a dam had burst and the things I'd pondered for months on end had come gushing out. Hearers began to invite people who were struggling with issues in their lives. Copies of the series were purchased and shared with others. God showed me yet again that human wisdom often falls short and only those who grow conversant in the language of low points can minister to a hurting world.

The Point of Low Points began with that series. I've excluded some of the material discussed in the sermon series and included other items to give this book the focus and the breadth needed to meet you where you are. I've also included a few personal experiences I believe will help you and small group participants to learn the lessons of the low points in our lives.

Although this book could be read in two or three hours, I urge you not to read it in such a manner. No gold stars will be granted for finishing this book quickly. A riverboat's maxim works here: rushing waters are not necessarily deep; still waters are often deceptively deep. Take the time to look up the Scripture references, make some notes, ponder what you're reading and make applications to your daily life. Let the words of this book lead you to a greater appreciation of the power of God visible in the low points of your life.

I don't strive to be eloquent in this book. Yet, many of the sentences in this book represent hours of seeking God's face and wrestling with my own wishes and wants. Truth sometimes sounds as a trumpet, but it can also come as a whisper. Tune your heart to hear the whisper of God when you read this.

And finally, I think this book should be shared. In coffee shops and over coffee tables, find fellow travelers in the valleys of life and discuss what you're reading and experiencing. The sections in this book along with the video sessions fit well in small group settings. Many people in your neighborhood or sphere of influence could benefit from a joint study and discussion of this book. You may wish to consider this.

This book has seven sections; the first opens the series with an understanding of the purpose of low points and an introduction to the life of Joseph—the man whose experiences will guide us through this study. The second and third sections introduce the first two low points in Joseph's life; the last three sections include the third, fourth and fifth low points.

The fourth section is my story and the background for this book. I call it, "In the Eye of the Storm." It's an interlude adding nothing to the narrative of Joseph's life or to the storyline as a whole. You may skip over it or you may wish to read it first. In this fourth section, I explain the low point that led me to look afresh at the life of Joseph. My church family walked with me through this low point, yet for one reason or another, I'm still unable to share some of the pertinent details of this trying time. I am painfully transparent with the emotions and thoughts I experienced during that time and catalog some of the changes God brought to my life. I pray it may help someone else who is going through a similar trial.

Thanks for joining me on this transformational trip. I believe you'll be glad you did.

SECTION I

VALLEY FEVER

CHAPTER 1:

THE FISHHOOK IN EVERY HEART

Adversity and humanity are synonyms.

A mother struggles to give birth to a child; a child struggles to be born. A fallen world welcomes another fallen man. Our days are few but seem marked with endless difficulties (Job 14:1). "God had one Son on earth without sin," opined Augustine, "but never one without suffering." All of God's children struggle and suffer.

Have you ever wondered why? Why is there pain? Why does adversity abound?

To ask why is to explore what has been called the "Achilles' heel" of Christianity. Achilles was the mythological character whose mother tried to protect him from a prophesied demise by dipping him as an infant in the River Styx. She missed a spot on one of his heels—the spot that an arrow later found. The problem of pain and suffering is the tender spot for people of faith.

Our reasoning goes like this: "If God loves me, then why has this happened to me?" Or, "If God is good, then why do bad things happen?" Or, still yet, "Since God is all-powerful, why can't He take away the pain?" From our childhood, we have been taught to pray, "God is great; God is good." His greatness and goodness should, to our way of thinking, eradicate our pain. But it doesn't and we are left wondering why.

God hears a lot of questions. Saul of Tarsus lifted sightless eyes and asked, "Who art thou, Lord?" (Acts 9:5). On the heels of that question, the future apostle Paul asked a second question, "Lord, what wilt thou have me to do?" (Acts 9:6). We ask the who, what, when and where questions of God frequently, but there is no question more pervasive and painful as why.

Christian author Lee Strobel commissioned a national survey that posed the question, "If you could ask God one thing, what would it be?" The most frequent response was, "Why is there so much suffering in this world?"

"Why?" It's the fishhook in every human heart. Sickness, disappointment, abuse, betrayal, broken relationships, sorrow, crime, accidents and a host of other troubles assail each of us.

> *Character cannot be developed in ease and quiet. Only through experience of trial and suffering can the soul be strengthened, ambition inspired, and success achieved.*
> *—Helen Keller*

And we ask the question, "Why did this happen to me?"

Made in His image, we seek to understand and perceive His ways. We want to know there is a reason behind what's happening to us—that life is more than fate, chance, or the roll of a dice. His way though is sometimes "in the sea" and His "footsteps are not known" (Psalm 77:19). Over the years, I've learned that we don't necessarily need to know why, but we need to know that there is a why. We must perceive that present sufferings work toward future glories (Romans 8:18-31).

What we know of God, however, keeps us from being cynical. We know that He is good and He created this world to be good (Genesis

1:31, I Timothy 4:4). Man's sin shattered the goodness, but God through His grace sought to restore fellowship with man. Suffering is not good, but God does His best work in those times when we hurt the most. Paul said, "All things work together for good…" (Romans 8:28). "All things" surely includes suffering.

Behind each and every low point in our life is a loving God working His will. If you're in a valley, it doesn't mean you made a wrong turn. It may mean that God has something for you. God shapes His best and chosen ambassadors in the valleys of affliction.

Through the odyssey of adversity witnessed by Joseph, we see that there is a point in each and every low point of life. By looking at his life, maybe our own lives will achieve greater clarity. We may not arrive at the place where we welcome adversity, but we may affirm with the songwriter, "In the valley, He restoreth my soul" (Dottie, Rambo. *Soul Classics*, 1968).

CHAPTER 2:

JOSEPH, THE "JESUS" OF THE OLD TESTAMENT

Why Joseph? What's so special about him that makes his life the subject of this study into life's valleys? These are good questions and deserve a response up front.

One reason we study the life of Joseph is that the opening book of the Bible devotes many of its chapters to him. The opening two chapters of the Bible describe the creation of the cosmos, Earth, and all living things including Adam and Eve. Two chapters comprised of sixty-six verses record the genesis of our universe. The Bible does not satisfy our curiosity regarding the Ice Age, dinosaurs, supposed missing links and the like. Without preface or qualifications, God's Word simply states, "In the beginning God…" (Genesis 1:1). This Book not only engenders faith; it requires faith.

Joseph's life is also found in the Book of Genesis. While the Creation may appear to get short shrift, the biography of Joseph is explored in fourteen chapters. Put that on the scales: Creation (two chapters, sixty-six verses) and life of Joseph (fourteen chapters, 448 verses). By a seven to one margin, Joseph's life is emphasized more than Creation. Such a Spirit-inspired emphasis cannot be ignored.

Heaven seems to suggest that it's more important we learn how to live than to learn how we were created. Origins are important, but character is essential. God's spoken Word created the world, but only faith in God transforms our worlds. Heaven shows us through Joseph how to recreate our worlds when they've been shattered.

Another reason we study the life story of Joseph rests in the meaning of his name. Names in the Bible are rarely random, especially in Genesis when the world was young. Since each word in Scripture is God-breathed, each name has significance and should be studied. This may seem a formidable task when you're plowing through the genealogies found in books such as I Chronicles or II Chronicles. Nevertheless, names do have meaning and should always be considered when studying the lives of men and women of faith.

Joseph was Jacob's eleventh son and Rachel's firstborn. Consider these two parents for a moment. Jacob, the future Israel, valued highly the things of God and had displaced Esau in the lineage of faith. In obedience to his father's commandment, Jacob purposed to go to his mother's homeland to escape the wrath of Esau and to find a woman to marry (Genesis 28). There he fell for his cousin Rachel, but his crafty father-in-law included her older sister, Leah, in the marriage mix. Jacob reacted to her deceptions by refusing to love Leah. And because Leah was unloved, God favored her with children. Leah conceived (Genesis 29:32) and in three successive verses, the same phrase is repeated three times, "she conceived again" (Genesis 29:33-35). Each child born to her sister was a dagger in Rachel's heart (Genesis 30:1).

God did not forget Rachel. After several years, through divine intervention, Rachel gave birth to her firstborn. She rejoiced saying, "God hath taken away my reproach" (Genesis 30:23). Rachel named him Joseph, saying, "The Lord shall add to me another son" (Genesis

30:24). Joseph's name means, "God will add." When Rachel spoke Joseph's name, she uttered a combined affirmation and supplication.

Rachel did not live to see what would become of Joseph. She died giving birth to a second son several years later. She did not live to see her firstborn ascend to power in Egypt and become the saving force for all of Jacob's family. Nor did she experience the many arrows of seeming misfortune her firstborn would endure.

John Ortberg posed an interesting question in his article, "Don't Waste a Crisis" (*Leadership Journal,* Winter 2011). He asked his readers to imagine they were handed a script for their newborn's entire life. They could see in advance each and every struggle the child would experience including learning disabilities in school, loss of a friend to cancer, car accidents, depression, loss of job and so forth. He then posed the question, "If you could erase every failure, disappointment and period of suffering, would that be a good idea?" After all, Ortberg concludes, "God isn't at work producing the circumstances I want. God is at work in bad circumstances to produce the me He wants."

Rachel was not given a script for Joseph's life, nor did she possess an eraser. She could not predict all that her boy would experience in life. If she could have, she would have used that eraser not once but many times. What parent wouldn't? Yet, the wisdom of erasing the low points can be called into question. For, the low

> *We were promised sufferings. They were part of the program. We were even told, "Blessed are they that mourn."*
>
> —C. S. Lewis

moments defined Rachel's elder son. In times of subtraction, he held to his identity of addition.

Years later, Rachel named her second child Benoni (son of suffering), but Jacob renamed him to Benjamin (son of power). Joseph's name, however, remained unchanged. His name gives precious insight into the point of all low points. Only through trials can God add His highest blessings to our lives.

A final reason we study Joseph is that he could rightly be called the "Jesus of the Old Testament." Numerous are the parallels between the lives of Joseph and Jesus: both were born in supernatural circumstances and were highly favored; both experienced rejection by their brethren and were sold for silver; both were tempted, but did not succumb to temptation; both saved people and were exalted and reigned. Some scholars have noted at least one hundred comparisons between Joseph and Jesus.

God wished to be seen early in the Bible. So, the first book of the Bible contains one of the most beautiful forerunners of Jesus Christ. Through Joseph, we gain a glimpse of the Jesus who was yet to come. The Law had not yet been chiseled into stone, but Joseph obeyed the Law. The Beatitudes had not yet been spoken in the Sermon on the Mount, but Joseph embraced them. We peer through Joseph into the ways and mind of God. We perceive God's blessings to come less through the traditional trappings of prestige, power, and prosperity; instead they came through the lowly accessories of humility, meekness, and poverty. We also perceive that God moves in the mundane to perform the miraculous. As God did with Joseph, He does with you and me.

Both Jesus and Joseph were curve-breakers. They defied the norm and moved beyond plains of mediocrity into the heights. People can, and often do, excuse their failure to live up to Christ's standard by claiming that Jesus was and is divine, whereas they are only human. Yet, Joseph was not God, but he was godly. Joseph was not eternal, but he made his life count. Joseph did not have twelve legions of angels at his disposal, but he managed with God's help to triumph over all adversity.

That's why we study Joseph. If he made it through the low points of his life with flying colors, then perhaps we can learn through him how to grow through life's ups and downs. We may also learn, like Joseph, to model Jesus to our generation.

God is more concerned that each generation sees Him than He is concerned with our convenience. That's a good thing to remember when moving forward in this book and in your life.

CHAPTER 3:

THE LAND OF HILLS AND VALLEYS

We humans like the fast-forward button. We like to skip over the tedious journey and arrive at the destination. More than once have we said, "Give me the highlights," meaning to omit the difficult details and share only the satisfying conclusions. We like to skip the mundane and arrive at the end of the book with all the issues clearly resolved. True life, however, isn't like that. The nitty-gritty must be lived and walked through.

It's easy to speak of the boy wonder known as Joseph—the favored child with a coat of many colors. He's the one who dreamed big dreams and lived to see his dreams come true. In our minds, we hasten to the moment in Joseph's story where Pharaoh sets him up as prime minister over the then most powerful nation of the world. The stuff in between, however, is what

> *Suffering has been stronger than all other teaching, and has taught me to understand what your heart used to be. I have been bent and broken, but I hope-into a better shape.*
>
> *Charles Dickens,*
> Great Expectations

led Joseph to this place. His disappointments, losses, and betrayals brought him to the place where he could emotionally, mentally, and spiritually grasp the amazing grace of our God. To omit the difficult moments in his life is to minimize the power of God and to gloss over what Joseph can teach us today.

Highlights require lowlights; high points compel low points.

Just before Moses died, he shared with Israel a description of the land God had promised to them. He called it a "land of hills and valleys" (Deuteronomy 11:11). Any visitor to Israel can attest to this description. We may even say that Moses was guilty of understatement. It's a land of dramatic changes in landscapes with high bluffs and deep gorges.

Many have viewed the Promised Land as a type of the world to come; yet it is less a picture of Heaven than it is a picture of the overcoming life. There were high points or blessings to be had. God promised the land would possess a sevenfold blessing of produce: wheat, barley, vines, fig trees, pomegranates, olive oil and honey (Deuteronomy 8:8). Egypt, the land of bondage, is credited with only six foods, six being the number of man: fish, cucumbers, melons, leeks, onions, and garlic (Numbers 11:5). There were seven feasts to be celebrated throughout the year in the Promised Land (Leviticus 23). The Promised Land was blessed!

But, it was also a land of valleys. The low points of adversity and struggle can be seen early. Jericho's walls had to fall (Joshua 6), a confederacy of five kings had to be subdued (Joshua 10), and the smorgasbord of thirty-one additional kings had to be consumed (Joshua 12). The battles did not stop there; the struggles continued.

God promised Israel the land, but possessing the promises took great struggle. It would be, "by little and little," the enemy would be driven from the land (Exodus 23:30). Sometimes the low points show we are passing through the portals into the land of fulfilled promises. God promised to take the Valley of Achor or Trouble and transform it into the doorway of hope (Hosea 2:15). Trouble is often the harbinger of a new day.

If we haven't already, we should quickly come to grips with the reality of low points in our lives. While we are thankful for the mountaintop experiences, we recognize our lives are not lived in the rarefied atmosphere of such unlimited vistas. Gravity is more than a law in the natural realm, it is a principle to be known and experienced in the spiritual realm. Look at Elijah. One moment, he's atop Mount Carmel standing alone against the false prophets of his day. A few hours later, we find the great prophet cringing in fear and depression beneath the shade of a myrtle tree. Sometimes, we're up; sometimes, we're down.

The path out of the valley appears when you choose to see things differently.

—Spencer Johnson, MD

I spoke a few years ago in the San Joaquin Valley area of California. The area, as you probably know, is where much of the produce in the United States is grown. I drove through clouds of dust kicked up by large tractors that were busy disking the fields. I didn't think anything of it until a few days later when I got very sick. One of my California friends gave me an advance diagnosis that a doctor later verified: *coccidioidomycosis*, or more commonly known as "Valley Fever." Fungus spores become airborne when the soil is disturbed. Those who live around the valley have built up immunity, but those unaccustomed to the area can be affected.

Strangers to the valleys in life can easily contract a spiritual valley fever. The symptoms can vary, but generally include: disorientation, anger, irritability, depression, isolation, self-pity, and hopelessness. Frequent visitors to the valleys of life will find these symptoms tend to recede over time, but initial exposure can threaten a person's walk with God.

I think we misdiagnose a lot of people around us. We desperately need the discernment possessed by the sons of Isacchar and promised by the Holy Spirit (I Chronicles 12:32, I Corinthians 12:7-10). People struggling around us may not possess a bad spirit or be guilty of some monumental offense against God; they may just suffer from valley fever. People who find themselves in a deep valley and suffering from valley fever don't require much. They just need a survival kit that includes a compass, an encourager, and the assurance that it's only a valley and not a box canyon...or, worse yet, a grave.

If you find yourself with a case of valley fever, first inoculate yourself against further damage by giving thanks. It is always the will of God to give thanks: both the high and the low points work together for good in our lives (Romans 8:28).

Alexander Solzhenitsyn received the Nobel Prize in literature for raising awareness of the forced labor system in Soviet prisons. He gave a firsthand account of his own years spent laboring in these prison camps. In his crowning work, *The Gulag Archipelago 1918-1956,* the author looks back on his life and pronounces a blessing on his prison experience. "Bless you, prison," wrote Solzhenitsyn, "for having been in my life!"

If we could gain access to the heavenly realm to interview former heroes and heroines of faith, we may be shocked to find them sharing a similar sentiment. The trials defined and refined them. Low points crystallized their thoughts and provided impetus to sharing the same.

Had the apostle Paul never been thrown into dungeons, much of the New Testament would be missing. Those low moments formed the inkwell of many sacred verses that we hold dear. From a prison cell, the great apostle reminded the Philippians that his experiences had rendered a miraculous transformation in his values: treasures became trash and losses became gains (Philippians 3:7-8).

A few years ago my family was privileged to travel to Europe. One of the greatest experiences we shared was to spend some uninterrupted time in the Sistine Chapel gazing at the glorious work of Michelangelo. The "Last Judgment" fresco dominates the sanctuary wall of the chapel. After gazing upon this fresco a while, I noticed that the saints depicted in Heaven clung to certain items. Andrew, Simon Peter, and Simon the Cyrene each hold crosses. Bartholomew holds his flayed skin. Catherine holds a piece of a broken wheel and Lawrence clings to a piece of gridiron. The life or death of each of these people was somehow associated with what they held in their hands.

A cross, a broken wheel, flayed skin and a gridiron—none of these can be called the mountaintop experiences of life. It's the valleys that define us and give us our identity. The low points reveal who we really are and who God is preparing us to be. Our valleys form crucibles in which God refines us.

Six psalms are given the title of "Michtam" in Scripture (Psalms 16, 56-60). Michtam means "golden" or "engraved in gold." Yet, each of these six psalms depicts the psalmist in dire straits. Four of the psalms add details that indicate these "golden" psalms were not written by David in his happier moments:

- Psalm 56: "Michtam of David, when the Philistines took him in Gath."
- Psalm 57: "Michtam of David, when he fled from Saul in the cave."

- Psalm 59: "Michtam of David; when Saul sent, and they watched the house to kill him."
- Psalm 60: "Michtam of David, to teach; when he strove with Aramnaharaim and with Aramzobah, when Joab returned, and smote of Edom in the valley of salt twelve thousand."

To be painfully frank with you, these titles make me tired just reading them. The six psalms begin with complaints or desperate pleas for preservation and mercy. The final Michtam is indicative of the psalmist's state of mind when writing these songs: "O God, thou hast cast us off, thou hast scattered us..." (Psalm 60:1). Strange stuff, it seems, to be called "golden."

One of the many superstitious practices that began in the medieval era was that of alchemy, the supposed art of turning lead into gold. Where the alchemists failed, the apothecary succeeded. David took the leaden moments of life and transformed them into the purest of gold. In the midst of each of these six psalms, a transformation takes place. Through faith and praise, David transformed his valleys into mountaintop experiences. In Psalm 55, David boldly declares in the face of betrayal, "As for me, I will call upon God; and the Lord shall save me" (vs. 16). In Psalm 57, the sweet Psalmist of Israel cries, "My heart is fixed, O God, my heart is fixed: I will sing and give praise" (vs. 7).

When David looked over the many dozens of psalms he penned and collected, he pronounced "golden" over six of them. Each begins with desperate pleas, but each ends with high praise. In the spiritual realm, lead can be transmuted into gold if you have the right materials.

Paul found this to be true and David likewise. As we look at the low points in the life of Joseph, may you also discover this to be true for your life.

For a special video from the author with additional information, please visit the following:

http://thepointoflowpoints.wordaflamepress.com/lpsection1

DISCUSSION QUESTIONS

SECTION I: Valley Fever

Author's Preface and chapters 1-3

Discuss the following questions:

1. The Book of Genesis spends far less time on the Creation than on the life of Joseph. Why do you think God placed more emphasis on Joseph's life than the beginning of life itself?

2. Joseph is sometimes called the "Jesus of the Old Testament." What are some of the parallels between the life of Joseph and that of Jesus? How do these parallel your own life?

3. Consider John Ortberg's quote: "God isn't at work producing the circumstances I want. God is at work in bad circumstances to produce the me He wants." Discuss how such a statement affects your view of life's low points.

4. Discuss the validity of the symptoms of a spiritual valley fever: disorientation, anger, irritability, depression, isolation, self-pity, and hopelessness. Are there any other emotions experienced in life's low points?

5. If you're in a small group setting discussing these questions, the facilitator will provide you with a piece of paper on which you will be asked to write down three or four of your life's lowest points. If you are reading this book without a small

group setting, take the time to make this list as well. Seal this in an envelope and write your name on the outside. You will open it again in the last session. But, before moving forward, pray that God will help you in the next few chapters to discover the meaning behind these low points.

SECTION II

JOSEPH'S FIRST LOW POINT: FACING LOSS

CHAPTER 4:

RACHEL WEEPS FOR HER CHILDREN

Joseph was probably six or seven years of age when he encountered the Promised Land. The twenty years of service his father had given to Laban were finished and the family made their pilgrimage to Canaan. Joseph had walked with his ten older brothers toward their Uncle Esau and, as instructed, bowed before this stranger. Young Joseph was probably old enough to understand that the encounter had gone better than feared. He was equally old enough to understand that his father was changed: he now walked with a limp.

After a skirmish in Shechem that Joseph probably didn't fully comprehend, his father announced that the family was going to Bethel. The young man watched in amazement as the household idols and jewelry were removed from houses and persons and stacked in the middle of the camp. Perhaps, his mother, Rachel, had told him that she had taken many of these idols with her from Mesopotamia, much to her father's chagrin. That was then. Now, the items once treated with great respect were piled unceremoniously in a heap. The entire hoard of treasure was buried in a deep hole beneath an oak tree. Joseph's father commanded all the family to bathe and put on clean clothes. By this, Joseph must have perceived the God of Jacob was of greater importance than Esau and was indeed a jealous God.

Joseph may also have seen a change in his father. The once happy-go-lucky, ambitious, self-sufficient man now limped slowly but determinedly down the road. Perhaps, he saw tears falling down his father's cheeks and noted the somber and respectful way he approached a certain mountain. When they arrived at Bethel, he perhaps watched as his father made a sacrifice. Maybe Joseph heard a rumble in the heavens, but Jacob heard the voice of God saying: "Be fruitful and multiply..." (Genesis 35:11).

Yet, to Joseph, there didn't seem to be any fruitfulness or multiplication. He watched as his grandmother's nurse died and was buried. But, that wasn't the only death. Someone far nearer and dearer to Joseph was to be taken from him.

En route from Bethel to Bethlehem (Ephrath), Rachel cried out in pain and went into painful, hard labor. Rachel's weeping could be heard across Bethlehem and became prophetic of another day when Bethlehem women would weep for their children (Matthew 2:18). The midwife assured her, "Thou shalt have this son also" (Genesis 35:17). Rachel's prayer was answered: Joseph, the child whose name was a prayer of addition, was to have a baby brother. The child lived, but Rachel did not.

Joseph and his ten older brothers had each been born in Mesopotamia, but only Benjamin was born in Canaan. God had brought Jacob back to Bethel, but in the midst of this period of consecration, he now lost his beloved Rachel. Joseph faced loss too—the loss of the land of his birth, the loss of the figurines and statues his mother had loved so much, and, most importantly, the loss of his mother. The tiny bundle held in the arms of a nursemaid somehow couldn't make up for the arms that would never hold him again.

Rachel was buried on the outskirts of Bethlehem. Jewish sages believe that each of the eleven older sons brought a stone to place on the grave. The stone Joseph brought could not have been large, but he probably found the biggest that he could. And as he added the rock to the memorial pile left by his mother, tears probably puddled down his face. For he alone of those piling rocks that day could truly say, "This was my mother." Maybe he added another rock for Benjamin. Conjecture aside, when Joseph turned his back to that grave, he was not the same. He had experienced a profound loss. The heap of stones represented the first low point in Joseph's life, that of loss. Joseph was at home with addition, that is after all, the meaning of his name. But, Joseph had been a stranger to loss until he turned six or seven years of age.

We may mentally grasp that there are seasons in life of gain and loss, of waxing and waning, and of exaltation and abasement. The writer of Ecclesiastes certainly grasped this fact (Ecclesiastes 3:1-9). The theory of loss, however, differs with the heart-wrenching, mind-numbing reality of loss. There seems to be no balm in Gilead for the pain of such loss. It stays with a person like a toothache, throbbing at the slightest provocation.

In April 2011, the online magazine *Slate* conducted an informal survey amongst its readers about grief and loss. About ten thousand people responded to the survey. A third of the people had lost someone close in the distant past, but they still sensed the loss. An equal percentage of respondents didn't feel like they could share their loss with anyone ("What is Grief Really Like?," Leeat Granek and Meghan O'Rourke, 4-28-11).

Loss clings to us.

One of the classic films of years gone by is *Citizen Kane*, which traces the life of a fictional newspaper tycoon from cradle to the grave. A newspaper reporter digs into the man's life to discover the meaning of Kane's last word: "Rosebud." Early in the film, viewers see a young Kane sledding in the snow in front of his mother's boardinghouse. Inside, Kane's mother is signing over guardianship of her son to get him away from an abusive father. Kane is pulled off the sled and hauled off to parts unknown where he seeks fulfillment and love in a variety of ways. He rescued a dying newspaper. He married, but left his wife for another woman. He became eminently successful, building an elaborate empire. But, he died largely forgotten with one thought in his mind and on his lips: "Rosebud." The film closes with the debris from the palace being shoveled into a furnace. The camera lingers on Kane's childhood toy lost in the debris, a wooden sled with a single word on its side: "Rosebud."

Many things may be forgotten in life, but not loss. It clings to us and we don't easily cast it off. Like the memorial to Rachel, losses accumulate over time: sullied reputations, discarded dreams, broken vows, estranged families, wandering prodigals, ruined fortunes, abandoned or stolen possessions, faded beauties and charms, memories, deaths, and chronic illnesses. The list seems endless. If the loss was caused by neglect or fraud, more salt is rubbed into the wound and the compounded hurt just doesn't seem to go away.

Until this time, nothing is said of Joseph's relationship with his father. After the season of loss, we read, "Israel loved Joseph more than all his children...and he made him a coat of many colours" (Genesis 37:3). After losing his mother, Joseph became the apple of his father's eye. He was drawn into his father's world and into his loving embrace. Like Jesus at the age of twelve, Joseph was now about his father's business.

Before we leave the subject of Rachel though, could I share one thought with you about her? She had prayed that Joseph would be the first of many children. In a way, God answered her prayer. Joseph's two sons were Ephraim and Manasseh (Genesis 48:5).

Benjamin had ten sons: Belah, Becher, Ashbel, Gera, Naaman, Ehi, Rosh, Muppim, Huppim, and Ard (Genesis 46:21). Her two sons had twelve sons and "all the souls were fourteen" (Genesis 46:22). The tribes of Benjamin, Manasseh, and Ephraim would one day camp to the west of the tabernacle during the pilgrimage to the Promised Land. They numbered 108,100 fighting men (Numbers 1:32-37). Joshua descended from Ephraim and the first king of Israel came from Benjamin. The apostle Paul, the greatest soul-winner who ever lived, hailed from the tribe of Benjamin. Rachel's prayers were answered. Ripples from her life continued to extend and expand long after she was buried outside of Bethlehem.

No loss is pointless. Although we may not seem to grasp it at the time or even during our time beneath the sun, there is an eternal purpose for everything that happens to us. Joseph's loss had the very real result of drawing him closer to his father. Our losses draw us closer to our heavenly Father. Could that not be the point of it all?

CHAPTER 5:

THE SUPPOSED GARDENER

I preached a few years back in the Tri-Cities area of Washington. The trip from Seattle through the Cascades to this agricultural area was enjoyable and restful. While driving through the rolling hills, I noticed what appeared to be diamond-shaped patterns of tree trunks dotting the landscape. Obviously it was an orchard, but I wasn't sure what had happened to the trees. Stopping at a convenience store to gas up the car, I asked someone about the orchards that seemed to be filled with fence posts rather than trees.

"Those are apple trees," the person told me. "Over time an apple tree will put on more bark than fruit. The only way to regain the fruit production is to convince the tree that it's dying. The tree is severely pruned so it will start producing fruit again."

The blind man once touched by Christ said, "I see men as trees" (Mark 8:24). A man's life is much like a tree. Over time, we put on more bark than fruit. It takes a gardener to remedy the problem of fruitlessness. His remedy does not just involve watering and fertilizing, he also uses pruning.

This occurrence took me back to when I first started pastoring the church in Pearland, Texas. To retain my CPA certification, I attended a continuing education class sponsored at a local school known for its architecture and arboretum. During a break in class, I walked along the well-manicured paths admiring the lush growth and careful landscaping. My admiration was short-lived. Rounding a bend, I saw what seemed to be destruction: limbs lopped off, plants uprooted, and debris strewn across the paths. I kept walking and around the next bend it was explained. A gardener stood astride the path with pruning shears in his gloved hands.

When Mary Magdalene first saw the resurrected Christ, she supposed Him to be the gardener (John 20:15). That's not a bad supposition. Mankind, after all, began his life in the garden. He also fell in the garden and was driven from the same. Jesus prayed in agony in the Garden of Gethsemane and was later buried in a garden. The church is called God's garden (I Corinthians 3:9) and God promises to transform His people from a desert to paradise, the "garden of the LORD" (Isaiah 51:3). Perhaps Mary Magdalene was correct in surmising Jesus to be the Gardener.

In this respect, the Gardener desires for His garden to be more than beautiful and fragrant, He

I asked God to spare me pain. And God said "No."
He said suffering draws me apart from worldly cares and brings me closer to Him.
I asked God to make my spirit grow. And God said "No."
He said I must grow on my own. But He will prune me to make me fruitful.

—Excerpted from "Love to Live," by Claudia Minden Weisz

wants it to be fruitful. In the great "abiding" chapter of John, Jesus plainly declared His desire for fruitfulness in His followers. Those who are not fruitful are taken away, but those who bear fruit will be pruned to bear more fruit. Jesus said that the Father is glorified if we bear much fruit, something that will happen if we abide (John 15:1-8). To a child of God loss can be explained, at least partially, by this simple fact: God prunes us to be more fruitful.

Think of this in the context of Joseph's life. His two parents are a study in contrasts. God's Word gives a three-word description of Joseph's mother: "Rachel was barren" (Genesis 29:31). The inability to conceive and bear children bears no stigma in our day, but in biblical settings it was humiliating to the woman. Many years passed before Rachel gave birth to Joseph, and several more years passed before Benjamin was born. Jacob, however, was abundantly fruitful. Jacob's father, Isaac, had blessed him with heaven's dew, the fatness of the earth, plenty of grain and wine, and that his brethren would bow before him (Genesis 27:27-29). Immediately prior to Rachel's death, Jacob's heavenly Father had changed his name to Israel and promised him fruitfulness and multiplication (Genesis 35:11).

Perhaps now is a good time to hit the fast-forward button. At the close of Jacob's life, he blesses all of his sons. Some of his blessings are thinly disguised rebukes, but when he comes to Joseph, the blessing is lengthy and full. His words begin like this, "Joseph is a fruitful bough, even a fruitful bough by a well; whose branches run over the wall" (Genesis 49:22). Jacob enumerates other blessings that sound very similar to the ones Isaac pronounced over him years before. He then closes by saying that the blessings of Jacob now rest upon Joseph (Genesis 29:25-26).

God had promised fruitfulness to one of Joseph's parents: Jacob. Joseph's loss of his mother brought him closer to his father. God, in effect, grafted Joseph more securely into the promised fruitfulness of his father, Jacob. Our thoughts are not God's thoughts. So, if we lifted this beyond the physical realm into the spiritual realm of advancement and Kingdom-mindedness, God permitted the loss of the good so Joseph could be drawn into the realm of the best.

Jacob fashioned a coat of many colors upon his son's shoulders. Jacob communicated his great love and affection. Only after Joseph's loss of his mother and his drawing closer to his father did the dreams come to him. Joseph dreamed as Jacob had dreamed. When others would mock Joseph's dreams, Jacob held his tongue for he knew the power of such dreams. Just as Mary would one day ponder the words of an angelic prophecy in Bethlehem's night skies about her firstborn son (Luke 2:8-20), Jacob must have contemplated the meaning of his favored boy's dreams. The loss of Rachel had pushed Joseph toward his father and into dream country.

God calls His children to fruitfulness. Thirty-, sixty-, and hundredfold blessings await those who will cooperate with His work. We don't mind the water bucket. We don't mind when God showers His mercy upon us. Yet, when His pruning shears appear, we cringe.

No one likes pain, but pain serves a purpose.

Biosphere 2 was built in the hills outside of Tuscon, Arizona, in 1987. The biosphere simulated five areas of this planet: rainforest, ocean with coral reef, mangrove wetlands, savanna grassland, and a desert. The designers intended this to be a prototype for how human beings would function in hostile environments, perhaps in colonies on the moon or distant planets. Over the next twenty years, the plants grew.

Expectations ran high and they were largely met. Yet, they fell short when it came to the trees planted in the biosphere. The expectation had been that the trees could grow tall and majestic without the hindrances of drought, pestilences, and heat of the outside world. The trees inside the biosphere, however, looked like no trees on the outside.

"Instead of growing straight and tall," observed Michael Dattalo who took a tour of the biosphere before it was closed, "the trees had grown bent, curving toward the ground as they grew, eventually leaning so far that they grew parallel to the ground, the leafy tops angling toward the earth. Without the braces and ropes that were attached to them holding the tops up, they would collapse completely on the ground." The tour guide explained to Dattalo's group that the merciless pounding of the wind against a tree's trunk that makes it strong enough to stand. "A tree without wind," said Dattalo, "is hardly a tree at all" (www.pcog.org/10427/a-tree-without-wind/, November 10, 2010).

It seems to be a rule of life: where life is the hardest, the strongest faith emerges. It's said that the finest violins are made from the trees that cling to the highest peaks. Where the winds are most severe, the sweetest music may be found. Gales are nightingales in disguise. From those supercharged furnaces heated seven times hotter than ordinary emerges the purest gold. Faith flourishes in affliction but languishes in ease.

Dr. James Dobson identified six child personality patterns used by children to cope with feelings of inferiority in his book, *The New Hide or Seek*. These six coping patterns are withdrawal, conflict, humor, denial, conformation, and compensation. When discussing the final personality pattern, he mentioned an intriguing study performed by Victor and Mildred Goertzel detailed in *Cradles of Eminence*. The researchers examined the lives of several hundred highly successful people including luminaries such as Franklin Delano Roosevelt, Helen Keller, Winston Churchill, Albert Schweitzer, and Clara Barton. Three-fourths of these people were raised in poverty, broken homes, or by rejecting, dominating parents. The overwhelming majority of the fiction writers (seventy-four of eighty-five) and poets (sixteen of twenty) came from homes in which serious psychological drama took place between parents. A quarter of these individuals suffered from severe handicaps such as blindness, deafness, and speech defects. Dobson credited these people with the remarkable gift of compensation, or the ability to realize that though they may have experienced loss in one area, they can excel in another area.

Human beings share many similar traits; not least among them is the learned ability to compensate. If the opportunity or inclination to excel in an area doesn't present itself, we look to another area. Should one door close, we seek an open door elsewhere.

The same God who opens doors also shuts them.

Such compensation can be seen in the lives of the men and women who ushered in the modern Pentecostal era. One of the founders of the modern Pentecostal faith, Charles Fox Parham, was very sickly as a child and struggled with sicknesses throughout his life. His well-known ministry of healing was born from his own personal struggles.

William Seymour of Azusa Street fame suffered from smallpox and lost vision in one eye. Seymour had also been raised in the oppressive Reconstructionist South and was searching for missing family members in the North when he came across a Holiness group called the Evening Light saints. Blind though he was in one eye, he caught a vision of what God could do through him.

Lucy Farrow is perhaps one of the most unsung heroes of early Pentecost, the first recorded African-American to receive the baptism of the Spirit in modern times. She was the niece of Frederick Douglass, and had been sold into slavery as a child and separated from her parents. Part of her adult life was spent traveling to Liberia searching for her relatives. She would go on to possess a great prayer ministry such that people patiently waited in long lines to have her pray that they might receive the baptism of the Holy Spirit. Howard Goss was one of those who stood in line to be prayed for by Farrow. She lived in a small apartment behind the Azusa Street Mission and fanned the flames of revival.

For this trio and many more, losses brought them in closer contact with their heavenly Father. They found in Him, the strength that they needed to not just survive, but to thrive. They did not faint; they flourished.

It's not everyday that three generations of loved ones are lost, but that happened to Jerry Sittser in the autumn of 1991. A drunk driver careened headlong into the minivan driven by Jerry and although he and three of his children

> *The most beautiful people we have known are those who have known defeat, known suffering, known struggle, known loss, and have found their way out of the depths.*
>
> *Beautiful people do not just happen.*
>
> —Elisabeth Kübler Ross

survived, he lost his wife, four-year-old child and mother in the crash. The grief from such a loss could have driven Jerry to despair, but he chose to compensate for this loss by sharing some profound reflections on grief and loss. In his book, *A Grace Revealed*, Sittser relates a question his son David asked him shortly after the accident. The eight-year-old David was the quiet one of the bunch, the least likely to discuss the accident. Driving to a soccer match one night, David suddenly blurted a question to his father, "Do you think Mom sees us right now?"

"I don't know, David," Jerry responded. "I think maybe she does see us. Why do you ask?" David said that he didn't see how his mother could see him. His reasoning was understandable: since Heaven is filled with happiness, then his mother couldn't possibly bear to see them so sad.

After some additional thought, Jerry responded, "I think she does see us. But she sees the whole story, including how it all turns out..." Then, the father added words that his son need to hear, "It's going to be a good story, David."

When Joseph found himself in the arms of his father, that's what he needed to hear. The story will continue and it will end up being a good story. We may not see the happily-ever-after down here, but we will see it someday.

Our heavenly Father sees the whole story. He knows the end from the beginning (Isaiah 46:10). His Word commands us to "train up a child in the way he should go" (Proverbs 22:6). The background for the Hebrew word for "train up" is agricultural. Gardeners train their vines to follow certain paths to grow more fruitful. So our heavenly Father trains and grooms us to become the person He wishes for us to be. It's what gardeners do.

Joseph's loss of his mother brought him in nearer proximity to his father and to the fruitfulness promised to his father. Our God is a giver; our enemy is a taker. God does, however, work through our losses to help those affected the most toward a certain future. God excels at beginnings (the first two chapters of Genesis), but God is equally great at new beginnings (the last fourteen chapters of Genesis). He redeems, starts over, transforms, and beautifies.

I tuned in recently to NPR (National Public Radio) and heard an essay read by John W. Fountain. Fountain is a journalist, a professor in journalism, and author who has Pentecostal roots. NPR asked him to write and read a short essay on the subject, "This I Believe." Fountain began his essay with four powerful words: "I believe in God...." For the next five minutes, Fountain described the God in whom he believed: the One who embraced him at four years of age when his alcoholic and abusive father was arrested; the One who warmed him when there was no heat in the freezing Chicago apartment; the One who held his hand when his teen peers were swallowed by hopelessness; the One who claimed him as His own son; the One who allowed him to feel His presence. When years later, standing before his natural father's casket, Fountain realized that in his father's absence, he had found another...or that his heavenly Father had found him.

Loss becomes gain in the Father's hands.

When Joseph turned away from his mother's grave, he found his father's arms to be open and welcoming. The next ten years would be marked with a strong bond developing between father and son—a bond that would not be broken in spite of others' efforts to do so. Rachel's name is almost absent from Joseph's adult biography. He probably thought about her often, but outside of the genealogies mentioning her in Genesis 46, her name would not be spoken again until Jacob was old, blind, and dying.

In his final days, Jacob rehearses to Joseph and his sons, Ephraim and Manasseh, how God promised him multiplication and fruitfulness while at Bethel. He declares that Joseph's two sons would also be named in his inheritance, effectively adopting Manasseh and Ephraim as his own (Genesis 48:3-6). On the heels of such weighty statements, Jacob brings up Joseph's beloved mother. Blind though Jacob was, he somehow perceived that Rachel's passing and Joseph's fruitfulness were connected. Such that when we read the many varying lists of the tribes of Israel in Scripture, we quite often find Joseph's name missing, but both of his boys, Ephraim and Manasseh, listed there (Numbers 2, 7, 10, and 34). Joseph was pruned, but had lived up to the meaning of his name, "God will add."

So, where does that leave us when we endure losses? When the Gardener prunes us, we should not perceive it solely as a loss, but we ought to recognize there will be a gain coming from it. The low point of loss is there to be faced, endured, and walked through knowing it will drive you closer than ever to your heavenly Father. And you will be the more fruitful because of it.

For a special video from the author with additional information, please visit the following:

http://thepointoflowpoints.wordaflamepress.com/lpsection2

DISCUSSION QUESTIONS

SECTION II: Facing Loss

Chapters 4-5

Discuss the following questions:

1. Rachel named Joseph "God will add." Discuss the power of speaking and praying in faith.

2. What percentage of our prayers do you think focuses on "addition"? What percentage of our prayers do you think focuses on "subtraction"?

3. Joseph lost his mother at a young age but was drawn to his father as a result. Can you think of a time in your life when a loss brought you closer to God?

4. The study called *Cradles of Eminence* reveals how renowned figures often "compensated" for their losses by excelling in other areas. Do you know of any personal examples of such compensation?

5. Pruning causes a fruit tree to yield more fruit. Describe any instance where the Lord permitted pruning in your life and the results that came from it.

SECTION III

JOSEPH'S SECOND LOW POINT: CONFRONTING CONFUSION

CHAPTER 6:

WHEN THE FORMULA DOESN'T WORK

I live along a saltwater lake that empties into Galveston Bay. While driving along the shoreline recently, I saw a sign that seemed funny to me. It read, "Jumbo Shrimp." An oxymoron is a figure of speech in which incongruous or seemingly contradictory terms are combined such as jumbo shrimp or active retirement. Each of these words appears in unlikely associations with their counterparts forming a willful disconnect to reality.

The same suspension of belief would be required for such phrases as: humble Herod, cruel Barnabas, or confused Joseph. Herod was anything but humble. Barnabas was an encourager and certainly not cruel. And, Joseph was not confused. Or, was he?

Joseph appears sure-footed in his biblical biography. Save for the sophomoric but understandable sharing of his vivid, God-given dreams with his father and brethren, one looks in vain to find Joseph making any mistakes. It's not that Scripture is willfully silent on human failures. Witness David's mistakes with Bathsheba and his numbering of Israel, and Simon Peter's denial of the Lord. The Lord ordered Joseph's steps and this young dreamer appeared to follow God's plan with precision—except on one occasion.

It's a little discussed facet of Joseph's life. I've never heard it preached about. No one dwells on it in Bible classes. In fact, we

51

skip over it because it seems of little import and because it's so
uncharacteristic of Joseph. There was a time, however, when Joseph
was confused.

His father called Joseph one day and instructed him to go to
Shechem to check on the welfare of his brethren and his father's
flocks. Joseph obeyed but when he arrived at Shechem neither his
brethren nor his father's flocks were evident. Scripture says that
Joseph was "wandering in the field." The Hebrew word for wander,
ta'ah, could also be translated as vacillating, going astray, staggering
as if intoxicated, or being misled ethically or morally. Joseph was not
strolling through the field in Shechem, he was staggering. Joseph
was confused.

The problem was he had obeyed his father's instructions without
the desired result. He had gone to Shechem, but his brethren weren't
found, leaving the young dreamer disoriented.

Confusion is that low point in life when the Father's word runs
out. We've done what we know to do and what God has told us to do,
but we haven't received the desired or promised result. Confusion
has reached epidemic proportions in our world. Scripture speaks of
the days to come when men's hearts fail them for fear, and if this
interval of time was not shortened, the very elect would be deceived
(Luke 21:26, Matthew 24:24). The "deceived elect" are two words
that shouldn't go together. Confusion brings unlikely associations into
our lives.

Much of our efforts beneath the sun attempt to prove a single
thing: that we are in control. We plan our lives, our finances, and our
retirements as if such things are within our control. We secretly believe
what William Henley wrote in "Invictus," that we are the masters of
our own fates and the captains of our souls. But as the old Yiddish

proverb says, "Man plans and God laughs." Any control we think we possess is illusory.

It's no accident I think that Joseph was looking for his brethren and his father's sheep. God's Word identifies us to be sheep, an unflattering but accurate description. Like sheep we are timid and easily confused. "All we like sheep," intones the prophet, "have gone astray" (Isaiah 53:6). Sheep are easily confused.

Some of God's creatures have a homing instinct that can zero in on the intended destination. Snails, cats, camels, salmon and pigeons possess such. We have frequently read of dogs lost hundreds of miles from home that patiently wend their ways back home. A sheep doesn't possess such an instinct.

A sheep can easily grow lost. Nibbling from one clump of green grass to the next, the sheep can get so preoccupied that she moves beyond sight of the shepherd and the flock. And once the sheep cannot see the flock, she is hopelessly lost. That's why the shepherd must go find her and bring her back.

Confused sheep are also vulnerable and easy prey for the enemy. When a sheep's fleece is full, it can easily tumble and be cast on its back. A cast sheep is unable to get up on its own and if left in this position it will grow distressed and die within hours.

Never is our confusion so great as when we are all alone. Think about those instances in Scripture when lonely people grew distressed: Hagar in Beersheba (Genesis 21), Elijah beneath a broom tree (I Kings 19), or John the Baptist in prison (Luke 7). Confusion confronts us when we are or feel alone.

Joseph was alone that day in Shechem. He staggered in the field not knowing what to do or where to go. But, even in this condition, the character of Joseph is obvious. When he reached the end of his father's word, he continued in that word until a further word came. He didn't strike out on his own. He didn't go his own way. He stayed in the field of Shechem going back and forth looking for his brethren.

We search for the formulas of a successful life. We think that if we do "A" followed by "B," then we should always arrive at "C." Such formulas usually don't work because they don't factor the "X" into the equation: God's sovereignty.

God doesn't always do things the way we think He should. The trip from Egypt to the Promised Land could have been made in eleven days, but it stretched out to a forty-year sojourn (Deuteronomy 1:2-3). God could have taken Israel the short way, but He "led the people about" (Exodus 13:18). His chosen path fulfilled a divine purpose.

It was not too long ago that the charismatic revival swept though many denominations. There was much to be admired in this revival and many people had genuine experiences with God. Coming from this movement also emerged many false formulas for achieving desired results: Holy Spirit baptism could be achieved by tongue-twisters; attitudes and misdeeds could be cast out as oppressive spirits; or the miraculous could be attained by following a simple series of steps. The "name it and claim it" rage swept the movement. Undoubtedly, some received what they sought; most, however, were disappointed and confused. The formula didn't work.

According to the US Bureau of Standards, a dense fog covering seven city blocks to a depth of a hundred feet contains less than a single glass of water. Fog is an apt metaphor for the feeling people sense when they are following the formula that isn't working. They are in a fog of doubt and confusion, not knowing for sure how they got there or how long it will last.

The advent of cyberspace has not helped matters. The Web provides an unending litany of promising formulas on how to accomplish various things. Frustration mounts as people try one formula after another only to see their best efforts fail. Confusion reigns supreme and people feel all the more hurt and lonely.

A Harvard valedictorian once said that the sum total of the college experience could be reduced to a single word: confusion. Contrary winds blow against us in these last days. Mixed signals from mixed multitudes abound. We hardly can hear the voice from behind that says, "This is the way, walk ye in it" (Isaiah 30:21).

Regardless of what one thinks about the Harry Potter books, the author's story is compelling. When the idea for Harry Potter came to Joanne Rowling, her mother was suffering from multiple sclerosis. Before three chapters of the first book were completed, Rowling's mother died, her abusive marriage ended, and she was forced to raise a daughter on her meager salary.

Years later, Rowling spoke to the Harvard Alumni gathering on "The Fringe Benefits of Failure." She said to the esteemed gathering, "Failure meant a stripping away of the inessential....Had I really succeeded at anything else, I might never have found the determination to succeed in the one area where I truly belonged.... Rock bottom became a solid foundation on which I rebuilt my life."

It's hard to imagine, but Shechem would be Joseph's "rock bottom." It's the only time in his life that he staggered and stumbled. Without this moment of confusion, however, he would have never known that Heaven shows up when we are at our most confused. He would have never discovered what God had for him.

These are unlikely associations: Heaven in the midst of our confusion; God in the midst of our failure. But, unlikely as it may seem, it is likely that God will be there when you are at your wit's end. He shows up.

CHAPTER 7:

THE AUTOBIOGRAPHY OF GOD

We left Joseph wandering in a field in Shechem. The Bible says a "certain man" found him (Genesis 37:15). Whenever Scripture speaks of a "certain man," our ears should perk up. For this phrase often describes a heavenly appearance by an angel or by God.

Years ago, Lloyd John Ogilvie, the former chaplain of the United States Senate, wrote a book entitled *The Autobiography of God.* He asserted that if you want to know God, you should look at the parables Jesus told. When Jesus described a "certain man" in one of these stories, He was actually describing God.

The phrase, "a certain man" is found thirty-two times in the King James Bible, split two-thirds in the Old Testament and one-third in the New Testament. Take the time to read the passages containing this phrase and your spiritual antennae will go up. The first mention of " a certain man" is found in the story of Joseph and that is not coincidental, but providential.

To the uncertain Joseph, the certain man comes. Some people conjecture that this encounter was Joseph coming in contact with his conscience: his true self. The Jewish scholar Maimonides suggests this was a messenger angel and other rabbinic scholars theorize that this was the first appearance of the angel Gabriel in Scripture. Still others believe this was the same heavenly being that appeared to

Joseph's father along the muddy banks of the Jabbok. More than a few scholars hypothesize that this certain man was an appearance of our Lord in the Old Testament. When the earthly father's word runs out, the heavenly Father speaks into our lives.

Joseph could have congratulated himself that he was in Shechem. This is where his grandfather, Abraham, sacrificed to God. However, nostalgia rarely holds the answer to life's present dilemma. Joseph's future was not in Shechem. He could have excused his wandering by saying he had followed his father's instructions to the letter. Yes, but the encounter with his brethren had not yet happened. He may have complained he had already come fifty miles. But, the certain man told him that he had fifteen more miles to go before he arrived at Dothan where his brethren awaited.

Earlier God had given Joseph dreams, but now God gave Joseph direction. Night visions are good, but daily direction is best.

Two gigantic columns graced the entrance to Solomon's Temple. The names of these columns are significant: Boaz (God gives direction) and Jachin (God gives strength). Each encounter with God is designed to give us direction and the strength to pursue that God-given direction.

I read a book recently that touched my heart entitled, *The Garbage Man Always Comes on Fridays* by Kristine A. Belfils. The small book was written by a married mother of two children who served as an assistant minister in a local church. She cared about people. She had a lot of hurt in her past and as is sometimes the case, hurt people know how to help people. A temptation in her past, however, came back to haunt her and she fell into the enemy's trap. She tried to escape but was again lured back into the same trap. The truth came out and she was forced to resign from the church and face the music. Lost in despair, she drove to a grocery store and purchased a large bottle of sleeping pills. She parked her car in a remote area of the lot and downed all the pills. When she finished consuming the pills, she phoned her husband and told him how sorry she was. She quickly lost consciousness, but help arrived in the form of EMTs and they saved her life.

When she was resuscitated, she expressed her sorrow over what she'd done. She returned home but things were no better. She beat herself over the head for her failures. On a day when she felt overwhelmed with sorrow, she heard the rumbling and familiar beeping of the trash truck coming down the street. A thought came to her, "That's the trash man. He always comes on Friday." And then a flood of emotion hit her. She said it was like her heart became a ringing bell. Just as certainly as the trash man comes on Friday, so too does Jesus rendezvous with the disappointing failures of our lives. As we roll our questions and heartaches to the edge of the street, He appears to faithfully answer our questions and gives us direction.

When the certain man found Joseph, he told the young man that he must go to Dothan. Did Joseph realize the turning point that was taking place in his life? Did he understand that the low point of confusion placed him in contact with a divine word? That a heavenly voice was speaking into his life?

I wonder if he questioned the certain man: "Will I see my father again?" "What awaits me in Dothan?" "What will happen to me?"

Joseph saw the sheaves and stars bowing to him, but there were things he did not see. He never saw himself staggering in Shechem. He did not see himself in a pit in Dothan. He could not envision being sold to a traveling band of Ishmaelites or stuck in a prison in Egypt.

That is, I think, the hidden part of every God-inspired dream. God allows us to see just enough of the future, to hear just enough direction and to receive just enough strength to move into our God-given purpose. But God is sparce with many details beyond that.

The certain man told Joseph what to do next: "Go to Dothan." So profound was Joseph's experience here that many years in the future, Joseph would command his brethren and children to bury him in Shechem. When Joseph looked back on his full and varied life, he must have valued that moment in Shechem more than all others; for then and there, he had his personal encounter with the divine. Jacob had his Bethel; Joseph had his Shechem.

As Joseph turned from Shechem to Dothan, he bid adieu to his childhood and his earthly father. He marched into his adulthood as directed by his heavenly Father. He accepted a God-given future for his life. If Rachel's passing was to draw him closer to his earthly father, Shechem and the emerging events were designed to draw Joseph closer to his heavenly Father.

Stop and think about this. If that "certain man" who met Joseph was indeed an appearance of God, then God directed Joseph to the place where his brethren betrayed him. God didn't skirt the skirmish, but pointed Joseph to the midst of it. Had Heaven instructed Joseph to return home from the field in Shechem, the next three low points in Joseph's life could have been avoided, but the dream would have never been fulfilled.

Dreams come with price tags attached. The greater the dream is, the greater the cost will be. Jacob's dream at Bethel carried a cost. Solmon's dream at Gibeah

> *Out of suffering have emerged the strongest souls; the most massive characters are seamed with scars.*
>
> *—E. H. Chapin*

came with a high cost. Paul had great unutterable visions, but he sacrificed and suffered much.

Jesus had a dream. He dreamed of a paradise lost being restored. He dreamed of wolves and lambs, lion and calves dwelling peacefully together. He dreamed of the world's curse being lifted and the earth being filled with the knowledge and the glory of the Lord. He dreamed of a world reborn and a resplendent bride dwelling in a magnificent city.

His dream came with a price. Jesus called it "the cup" that He must drink. The awful costs of redemption were clear to Jesus. Without the shedding of blood, there would be no remission of sins and no future for mankind. No one took his life; He laid it down willingly. Beyond Calvary and the empty tomb, He still carried the scars with Him. Had he not chosen to go the extra mile and climb Golgotha's hill, the dream could not have been given life.

Four centuries ago, John Bunyan introduced to the world some memorable characters on their way to the Celestial City. There came a day when Bunyan's Mr. Valiant-for-Truth received his summons to pass over the chilly waters into the gates of splendor. He called for his friends and told them he was headed to the Father's House: "…Though with great difficulty I have got hither, yet now I do not repent me of all the trouble I have been at to arrive where I am. My sword I give to him that shall succeed me in my pilgrimage, and my courage and skill to him that can get it. My marks and scars I carry with me, to be a witness for me that I have fought His battles who will now be my Rewarder" (*Pilgrim's Progress*, Part 2).

Hidden costs bring open reward. That seemingly chance encounter in a field at Shechem did something for Joseph. As surely as he pursued his father's word to Shechem, he now pursued his heavenly Father's word to Dothan. Joseph's knowledge that he had encountered the divine and had received direction would see him through the upcoming trials.

When the "certain man" appears in your low point, you can go on the strength of that encounter for a long time. It is my prayer that your story will intersect with His story and that history will be made.

The same God who spoke into the night and chased away the darkness will speak into your world. The confusion vanishes. The fog lifts. And you see abundantly clear what you must do.

For a special video from the author with additional information, please visit the following:

http://thepointoflowpoints.wordaflamepress.com/lpsection3

DISCUSSION QUESTIONS

SECTION III: Confronting Confusion

Chapters 6-7

Discuss the following questions:

1. Jews believe the "certain man" who appeared to Joseph was actually God. Discuss how God often appears to people when they are confused.

2. How difficult do you think it was for Joseph to trust in the word of an unknown stranger? How does his obedience relate to our trust in God?

3. Why do you think God's Word frequently compares us to sheep?

4. What conclusions can you draw concerning God and His house from the fact that the columns gracing the entrance of Solomon's Temple were called Boaz (God gives direction) and Jachin (God gives strength)?

5. How often do you think people give up on a dream because they encounter low points of confusion and despair? What advice would you give to them?

INTERLUDE

THE EYE OF THE STORM

CHAPTER 8:

SOME RAIN MUST FALL

Striking, disturbing images from Hurricane Sandy's landfall in the northeast United States swept the country. Tidal surges, gale force winds, rain, and snow lashed the most densely populated area of this nation, an area accustomed to difficulties, but unused to the devastation wreaked by such storms. The storm left many people without power, food, water, transportation, proper clothing, and heat.

Some low points are reached in such a sudden manner. Storms—physical, relational, financial, and spiritual—come fast and can stay long.

When I first began pastoring in the late 80s, a friend recommended H. Becker Hicks, Jr.'s *Preaching through a Storm* to me. Hicks described his first years pastoring the Metropolitan Baptist Church in Washington, DC. Everyone, including pastors, face difficulties in times of transition. To paraphrase the wise Solomon, exits and entrances are life's toughest things (I Kings 3:7). Winds of unrealistic expectations, high pressure systems of stress, and the tidal forces of unexpected crises whip up genuine storms during times of transition. Hicks was in a storm and he did what all preachers have done down through time: he preached his way through the storm.

Hicks described some of the difficulties he faced in pastoring a church established since the Civil War and transitioning it to be a viable congregation in a new century. The proverb proves true: the old going out always fights the new coming in. Hicks could testify to the truthfulness of the proverbs.

Some storms in life are avoidable. The Apostle Paul told the captain of that ill-fated vessel to not set sail for the intended destination. He clearly identified the consequences of such an action: shipwreck, loss of cargo, injuries, and danger to all on board. (See Acts 27:10-11.) The captain, however, insisted they depart and the ship sailed into the midst of a fourteen-day storm. In our lives some storms are avoidable, but once we are in the storms whether they could have been avoided brings precious little solace. We only hope to survive the storm.

I read Hicks' book my first year of pastoring. I tucked it away and thought, "I appreciate the honesty and the sincerity with which he approached this storm." In many ways, I've lived through such storms and am certain there will be more to come. Storms have the habit of removing those tissue-thin facades and pretenses. Storms make us real. When Hicks received his call to leave one historic church in Houston, Texas, and travel to our nation's capital to pastor another historic church, he said that a storm hit Metropolitan Baptist Church and shook the building with thundering and lightning. The storm became an apt metaphor for all that Hicks endured over the next several decades.

After sharing some of his pastoral experiences, Hicks introduced the first sermon of the book based on the text: "Weeping may endure for a night, but joy cometh in the morning" (Psalm 30:5). He called the message, "How Long the Night?" Toward the end of the message, Hicks preached:

I know there's a better day a coming, but how long is the night?
I know one day every day will be Sunday and every month the month of May, but how long is the night?

I know "God moves in mysterious ways His wonders to perform," but how long is the night?

I know "all things work together for good for those who love the Lord," but how long is the night?

I know I need to "wait on the Lord and be of good courage," but how long is this night?

I know "Jesus is near to comfort and cheer just when I need Him most," but how long is my night?"

I know that "earth has no sorrow that heaven cannot heal," but how long is my night?

I know "there's a bright side somewhere," but I still need to know how long the night!

(*Preaching through a Storm*, Zondervan, 1987, pp. 30-31).

I was mesmerized with the cadence and content of the message. I was intrigued with how Hicks' preaching was affected by the storm he endured. I learned a lot of lessons through that book that I would relearn in the years to come. Storms change us and shape our message to the world. The sermon ended with a ray of hope that Hicks perhaps didn't feel so early in his storm, but he shared it anyway: that God has the curious habit of showing up in the midst of our struggles.

As a young pastor, I tried preaching a similar message. It fell flat, as it should have. It wasn't my story; it was his story. Only those who come through the storm have the right to preach such a message. "This is my story!" is more than an opening line to the chorus of a beloved hymn; it's the singular voice of triumph that emanates from the person who has survived the storm and received revelation.

My storms did come and gave me my story. I learned early, however, that few in life's audience seemed interested in hearing my story. On those rare occasions I spoke of my trials, to my own ear, I sounded like I was complaining or, worse yet, looking for pity. Another major storm hit ten years into my pastorate; but no one wanted to listen. We are, at times, good at rejoicing with those who rejoice; but we are poor at weeping with those who weep. So when the storm came in 2008, I knew that everyone was wrapped up in their own worlds and whatever comfort and strength I would find would be with God, my wife, my family and a few trusted confidantes. As with preceding storms, I largely entered the quiet zone. Nothing spoken in public; heart emptied in private. Silence is not golden to any believer, but most especially to a preacher.

Perhaps you are in an unavoidable storm, a storm not of your own making. I feel for you. I weep with you. Or, you may be in an avoidable storm, a storm of your own making. I feel for you as well and I weep just as sincerely. For I know that the latter type of storm heaps the flotsam and jetsam of oppressive guilt and stinging regret. Storms, avoidable or unavoidable, bring untold damage and should prompt the same response from those who care.

As I write this, I just got a text message from a young husband in our church. He and his wife have wanted a child for so very long and their dream seemed realized a few months ago when they received news that she was expecting a child. Joy turned to sorrow today when the doctor said, "The baby's heartbeat has stopped." The text stated that they wanted no visitors, only prayers. My wife and I prayed for the young couple and later I told her, "We weep with you. We know that God sees and His great heart breaks for you. And that even in the midst of this, though we don't yet see how, He will make all things beautiful. Grow strong in the comfort and knowledge that He is at His closest when we are at our weakest."

Where did those words originate? Not from a book, but from personal experience. Personal storms teach us some vital things that can and must be shared. Paul said that God comforts us during our trials so we may comfort others who are enduring similar trials (II Corinthians 2:1-4). Storm-taught lessons can perhaps help others form the bulkheads and seawalls to protect their hearts and minds from utter devastation. At the very least, the counsel of others who have shared our experiences is a prized scrap of blue tarpaulin to partially shelter you from the storm. It's worth much to know that others have been there and that they somehow survived. Hope is an essential force in a storm survival kit.

This series, *The Point of Low Points*, was born of personal experience. "Not to transmit an experience," advised Elie Wiesel, "is to betray it." Yet, Wiesel's trip through the Holocaust made my experience pale in comparison. Overcoming my initial reluctance to sharing these lessons was difficult, but God pressed me. We believe; therefore we speak (II Corinthians 4:13). At first, I shared only bits and pieces of this story to gauge peoples' reactions. I was surprised. People seemed like they wanted and needed to hear what I learned. So, I share with you what happened in hopes that a clear message will get through to you: no matter what you're going through, you are going through. You cannot and will not quit. You must see it through the storm.

During the storm experience, my most favorite song became one written by Charles Aaron Wilburn and Bill and Gloria Gaither entitled "It Won't Rain Always."

> *Someone said that in each life some rain is bound to fall,*
> *And each one sheds his share of tears,*
> *And trouble troubles us all.*

But the hurt can't hurt forever
And the tears are sure to dry.

And it won't rain always.
The clouds will soon be gone.
The sun that they've been hiding has been there all along.

And it won't rain always.
God's promises are true.
The Son's gonna shine in His own good time
And He will see you through.

Gospel singer Janet Paschal sang this song after going through her own personal storm: a bout with cancer. When the sky is dark and the winds and surf are raging, it's good to remind yourself that it won't rain always. This too shall pass.

How long is the night? Not much longer. Hold on.

CHAPTER 9:

THE STORM COMETH

In September 2008, my world was upended. Not just mine, but also the lives of many people in the Houston area were inalterably changed. The source of change was a storm named Ike. While the world may measure time with BC and AD, I don't think I'm being too dramatic to say that BI and AI soon segmented my life: Before Ike and After Ike. Before Ike, life was good or at least I like to tell myself that. After Ike, the world did not seem so good. In fact, my world collapsed.

Ike began as a Cape Verde-type hurricane, which is not good. The worst storms to hit the US coastline typically originate around this island chain off the coast of West Africa. The Great Storm of 1900, which still ranks as the greatest natural disaster in US history, was born in the same place and was eerily similar to Hurricane Ike. The long distance and the warm waters gave Ike a chance to grow. And, grow it did until it filled the Gulf of Mexico with its tidal surges and tropical force winds. Its path varied little once it entered the Gulf. Like the 1900 storm, Ike made a beeline for Galveston, Texas, where this Category IV hurricane ultimately made landfall.

I pastor in a place called Pearland, the second-largest suburb of Houston, situated between this fourth-largest city of the United States and Galveston. As the crow flies, our town is ten miles from Galveston Bay and the church I pastor is only about thirty feet above sea level.

We did not escape the ravaging effects of the storm. Several of our families lost their homes, some to floodwaters, some to high winds and others to fire. None of the church family lost their lives and for this blessing I was truly thankful.

Ike is the storm that never stopped. The storm came ashore on Friday night and Saturday morning, September 12 and 13. The devastation was immense. On Monday, September 15, as the last of Ike's winds were passing over the Great Lakes region into Canada, a storm of a different sort hit New York City. Lehman Brothers, the financial services firm, filed bankruptcy—the largest bankruptcy in US history. The Dow Jones dropped five hundred points and the ship of State was loosed from its financial moorings. The unraveling of the economy coupled with the storm wreaked untold havoc on our damaged church.

The church had relocated to its present address ten years before Ike arrived. Millions of dollars were spent to transport our church from its original neighborhood setting to a choice location along the main highway traversing our city. The church had grown in the past decade and was, to my way of thinking, doing well.

Ike proved me wrong. The physical church structure was severely damaged by the storm. Although the hatches had been battened down before the storm with doors and windows secured, it appears that a tornado came close to the building sheering utility poles, pulling the doors open, and collapsing the awnings and porticos. Hurricane-force winds with all manner of storm contaminants blew unfettered through the building for hours. The main roof blew outward and assumed the appearance of a risen loaf of bread. Ike brought ten to fifteen inches of rain and the interior of the building was saturated with water and storm contaminants.

My immediate attention after the storm abated was fixed on finding our people to determine if they were unharmed and doing as well as could be expected. Once we were satisfied that the church family was safe and their pressing needs were met, our attention turned to the building itself. Volunteers came to the church to help clean up the storm debris and stretch those blue tarpaulins, so familiar to those who have been through storms, across the damaged roof. The pastor and family of a new church plant in Galveston relocated behind the church and helped with the cleanup. Their hearts were broken over their loss, but Ike became for them, the open door to minister to a broken city. To date, they've baptized about one thousand people since Hurricane Ike. Storms, on occasion, can bring needed revival to an area.

There was no power in our part of Houston for eighteen days. The interior of the church was muggy; the carpets and floors were mushy; and the air smelled like hurricane—an unpleasant and offensive aroma borne of the microbial, environmental contaminants in the storm water. Oppressive is an apt, one-word description for the atmosphere of the church. We hired a vacuum service that began the tedious process of extracting water from the building. After a few attempts, we located diesel generators big enough to power-up the building. We intermittently powered up isolated areas of the church in a futile attempt to dry the building out.

My wife and family had evacuated to Austin, Texas, during the advance of the storm. After the storm passed, my habits became familiar. I drove to Pearland daily in the wee hours of the morning and would return to Austin in the evening. I purchased groceries and transported them to Pearland for the people in our church and community. There was no food to be had in the Houston area. Our church leaders and volunteers set up grills and cooked what they could. Cars lined up by the hundreds on the highway in front of the church to collect the free food. People were desperate. If people needed ice, they went down the street to the Baptist church and waited in long lines. If they needed water, they waited in equally long lines at the FEMA distribution points.

I'll never forget my first trip to the building after the storm. There were no traffic lights or streetlights. Airports were closed down. Downtown high-rises stood dark and empty. Shelves in grocery stores were bare. If a gas station had fuel and the power to pump the fuel, hundreds of cars would be in line to fill their tanks or gas cans.

Storms reveal how weak and vulnerable we really are.

Before nightfall, I would exit the city for the return trip to Austin. It was too dangerous driving on streets that had no traffic or streetlights. Back and forth I went those first few days after the storm.

The first week slipped by with me being secure in the knowledge that everyone in the church had survived the storm and the property was insured. More than once I said, "Well, at least we have insurance! Stuff can be replaced." My cavalier, Pollyanna mindset would soon be tested.

Seven days after the storm, the insurance adjuster came to the church to inspect the damages. The church family was serving hungry people on the parking lot that day as he inspected the building. I'd almost forgotten he was there when he caught up with me in the afternoon and asked to have a word with me. As we walked away from the crowd of volunteers, I began to rehearse with him some of the planned steps for further mitigation: additional generators, dehumidifiers, and so forth. He stopped me, and nearly stopped my heart, with his next words.

Replaying these words in my mind five years later is difficult. But, to the best of my recollection, the adjuster said, "Pastor, it's useless to mitigate further. The water saturation has been too immense. You are going to have a mold problem in this building. Once you get power up to the building, I need you to demolish the interior."

You could have knocked me over with a feather. The ramifications of what he suggested were beyond what I could fathom. I remember thinking to myself, "Where will the church meet for services? How long will this take? What will be the effect on our church family?"

While my mind was whirling, the adjuster spoke words that resonated with me for many years. "Pastor," the adjuster continued, "take this church back to the steel and stone."

Back to steel and stone...

CHAPTER 10:

TAUGHT BY THE STORM

"Back to steel and stone…"

The moment the adjuster said these words I sensed the voice of the Holy Spirit speaking to my heart. How long had it been since we made the journey back to the foundation of what the local church should be and who God called us to be? I had pastored the church at the time for twenty years and thought that we had achieved a lot. I sensed at that moment, however, the unfailing and unflinching eyes of the Lord inspecting our efforts, and I sensed as well that we had come up short of His expectations. Worse still, I felt that we had somehow let God down.

The next few days were a blur. My confidantes told me that this was good news, that the insurance carrier had stepped up to the plate and was taking responsibility for restoring the building. I was soon disabused from this idyllic notion. Word came that a supervisor of this adjustor had shown up on the property and was talking down his underling's report. The adjustor disappeared never to be heard from again. The one who took his place seemed determined to minimize the damages and maximize the delay. So began the long slog of fighting the carrier to restore the building began—a trial that has now extended five years.

Since we had no clarity from the carrier as to what would be covered and repaired, we determined to make do with what we had. We continued to dry the building out and before we had power fully restored, we began holding services again. This continued through the winter of 2008-2009 as we awaited word on how to proceed. The carrier had gone 180 degrees from the first adjustor's assessment and was actively fighting payment on the claim. A particular low point for me was when we had to pay thousands of dollars to an out-of-state engineer to prove that a hurricane had hit Houston, something that was obvious to all. We had to pay to prove the storm had come— not the first time people who have suffered have been forced to prove it to skeptics.

All the while, something was growing in the building. From the outset, I communicated to the carrier through the professionals we retained to represent our interests that there were certain odors in the building that indicated storm contaminants and mold. Across Houston, swimming pools were filled with black mold caused by Hurricane Ike. Trees around the church were covered with the same toxic contaminants and began to perish. I feared something similar had permeated our church.

A full six months after the storm, air quality testing was finally ordered. The results were not surprising, at least to us. Black mold and other contaminants were throughout the building. During those months, I went into the office feeling good, but within hours I felt sluggish, feverish, and confused. The air quality test results showed an unusually high invasion of the penicillin bacteria in my office, something to which I'm highly allergic. Black mold and other microbial growth were found throughout the church. Soon the church became off-limits. We were told to worship elsewhere.

Where would we go? We owned a family life center two miles down the street. It had been moderately damaged by the storm and had not yet been repaired, but it would be a familiar and suitable place to hold services. Our church leaders wrestled with this decision. We already knew to rebuild the sanctuary would require every penny we could save, raise, or borrow and we had a buyer for the family life center, howbeit at a discounted price. After a lot of soul-searching, we decided to sell the family life center to get a down payment on the reconstruction of the sanctuary. The local school district offered us an old auditorium at one of the junior high schools. We were thankful to have a place to go.

The auditorium was pricey to rent but beggars can't be choosers. Over the next year I would often say, "We have heating and air conditioning: heating in the summer and cooling in the winter." Winters are never hard in South Texas but that one was colder than most. Few uncovered hands were lifted in worship that year. It looked like a sea of mittens when we praised God. The entrepreneurial spirit captured our youth and they began selling hand-warmers and foot-warmers in the lobby. Summers were tougher. The high heat and humidity rendered the auditorium nearly unbearable. Doors were propped open and box fans were placed in front of them to stir the hot, humid air. In spite of it all, we were still thankful for a place to worship and forever owe a debt of gratitude to a school district that opened its arms to us.

My first sermon to the congregation in exile was a gritty affair. I began by saying, "Welcome to our sojourn in a strange land. I'm reminded of the seventy souls of Jacob's family that went into Egypt. What they faced was tough, difficult and oppressive. But, when they left they were over a million strong. May God smile on us during this time!" This cheerful opening soon dissolved into the grim recognition that coming to church was no longer going to be so convenient.

Our pride suffered the most—well, make that my pride. Within weeks, I grew alarmed as the numbers in the congregation dropped. Inconvenienced and unsure of the future, many families started seeking for greener pastures. To my own way of thinking, I thought these might have been the brightest among us. I stopped looking at attendance and financial reports. Ignorance may not be bliss, but at times it's much less painful.

Doubts assailed me. My heart and mind became a question-mark factory. What was happening? What would the future hold? Was God going to have a church in this city?

Please be aware that when the church seems to be going good, it's my tendency to call it "my church." When things start going south, I cheerfully pass ownership over to God and start saying, "What will you do with your church?" One thing God taught me during this time is that the congregation I pastor is His church, in both the good and bad times.

Back to steel and stone...

With a "what-have-I-got-to-lose" mindset, I started preaching what I now call "Back to the Rock" messages. I preached Jesus every way I could figure. I taught doctrine. I challenged the remaining folks to commitment, consecration, and separation. The apostolic blessings of vision, faith, and the miraculous were displaced with the more needful staples of sacrifice, prayer, and devotion.

It seemed to me then, that God had provided the tenor of the message. Low times demand deep messages. "Rend your heart" Joel advised, "not your garments" (Joel 2:13). In difficult seasons, empty calories won't do; only bread from above suffices.

I came across an old book recently that contained the sermons of the Scottish Reformers who went up against the entrenched religious hierarchy. They were persecuted, ostracized, and killed.

This bit of history became known as the "Killing Times." The persecuted preachers of those sermons were profound in their clear-eyed vision of the difficulties of the season, but they were equally optimistic that God would bring them through. Faith is not ignoring the difficulties, it is recognizing that God is bigger than the obstacles we face.

I was in a "Killing Time," but I prayed that I wasn't killing time. Over the next several months, a spiritual dismantling took place. Our church structure fell apart, partly because there was inadequate space to fully operate any ministry. Organizational charts became populated with empty boxes; job titles were few and far between. Staff meetings proved no longer necessary; there was nothing to talk about. An abiding symptom of low points is silence...or soft weeping. That was being heard in the hallways of the school auditorium. With no accessible prayer room, we stood or knelt on hard, cold terrazzo floors and cried out to God. When desperate, the conducive and comfortable are no longer required.

> *Amidst the confusion of the times, the conflicts of conscience and the turmoil of daily living, an abiding faith becomes an anchor to our lives.*
>
> *—Thomas S. Monson*

Back at the church property the demolition slowly continued. The area was quarantined and marked with biohazard symbols. The process became repetitive: hygienists marked the areas to be demolished; workers demolished only to find more infected areas; delay and debate about the extensiveness of the area to be removed; the quarantine barriers were rebuilt and the entire room was demolished; then, on to the next area. Slowly nearly forty thousand square feet of building were being taken back to steel and stone.

At night, I would don protective gear and slip into the sanctuary. There where laughter, worship, preaching, and music had once been heard, only the sound of air scrubbers hammering through the hollowed building could now be heard. Each time I slipped in there, I tried my best to look beyond what was and what had been to what might be some day. Admittedly, it was difficult to do. I modeled what I had learned from my elders. I prayed; I wept; and then I worshiped. I danced all over the sanctuary floor saying, "Not always, Lord. Not always. It will not always be like this. Only through You can we come out of this."

If the moon, our planet's nightlight, can rise high in the darkened skies and exert her gravitational pull on the oceans many miles away, I reasoned that I could do the same through worship. If somehow I could separate myself from my present ordeal and be lifted into the presence of the Lord, maybe I could gain perspective and maybe it could somehow influence my ongoing chaos.

I did my best imitation of Job telling God that He gives and He takes away, but I would still bless His name. Frankly, my attestations fell flat and I failed to convince myself, much less the One who knew my heart and every thought. But, I tried. Oh, how I tried!

Toward the end of that first dismal, oppressive summer I was pretty beat up. Close to the first anniversary of Ike, I preached "What God Will Not Do." God will not extinguish a flickering candle; He will not break a crushed reed (Matthew 12:20). By this time, I was clinging to the character of an unfailing God. As the legendary healing herb called alethas found only in the king's hands in Tolkien's *Lord of the Rings*, I knew then that only God held my answer.

I found myself in the same predicament described by psychologist Larry Crabb in his book *The Pressure's Off.* He described how at the age of three he had locked himself in a second-floor bathroom. He was hysterical with fear and began sobbing and pounding on the bathroom door. His father acted quickly and decisively. He placed a tall ladder outside the house and soon his face appeared in the window silencing the sobs within. He pried the window open, crawled through and unlocked the bathroom door. Crabb said he remembered saying, "Thanks, Dad." A few moments later, the three year old ran downstairs and outside to play.

The author suggests that this is how we believe the Christian life to work. We can't get out; God shows up to get us out. But in actuality that's a three-year-old's faith. As an adult, we are faced with many locked doors—wounds that won't heal, marriages that don't work, rebellious kids, traitorous friends, dying ministries, and lonely feelings that won't go away.

"God has climbed through the small window into my dark room," Crabb writes. "But He doesn't walk by me to turn the lock that I couldn't budge. Instead, He sits down on the bathroom floor and says, 'Come sit with me!' He seems to think that climbing into the room to be with me matters more than letting me out to play."

> *As you walk through the valley of the unknown, you will find the footprints of Jesus both in front of you and beside you.*
>
> —*Charles Stanley*

In the low points of life, I had to have more than a three-year-old's faith. I needed a full-grown faith that could celebrate the God of the shut door.

Sometimes God calms the storm; and sometimes He calms the person in the storm. More times than not, the latter option seems to be His preferred course of action. God seems to think that His presence is better than the storm's absence.

I remember watching as the remediation company removed objects from the church. One of the items removed was a tract rack we kept in the hallway of the church. Although hurricane-force winds had coursed through that hallway and immense amounts of water had flowed across the rack, some of the tracts survived the storm. I could just make out some of the titles: "The Apostles' Doctrine," "The Way We Worship," and "Contending for Modesty." As I watched the tract rack with its few remaining tracks leave the premises, I remember saying, "I still believe. God, I still believe."

Somewhere in the deepest part of this wilderness experience, the most surprising thing happened: the church numbers stopped plummeting. Then, something even more

One of the necessary components is that those [turnaround] churches brought in a new individual to be their primary leader, and that individual is not just a preacher-teacher— not that that's bad, we need those—but that the individual who came in to spearhead that ministry was first and foremost a leader.

—George Barna, Homiletics *interview*

miraculous happened: the church began to grow. Dedicated people whose hearts beat with mine started showing up for services.

Banks refused to loan us money because of the new TARP (i.e., Troubled Asset Relief Program) regulations passed shortly after the financial collapse. We paid what we could from the church treasury and from the proceeds of the discounted sale of the family life center to get the building restored, but we only had enough money to make a small showing on the building. A bank stepped forward at that time and loaned us the money to continue the rebuilding project. The building started to take shape.

Our church had turned around, that alone was a miracle. I once read a book by George Barna called *Turnaround Churches* where the author noted that 80 percent of all churches are in a state of decline. He also wrote that in nearly all cases where the decline was stopped it came through a new leader with a new vision. Our church had not only turned around, but it had done so with the same pastor. Yet, to be frank, perhaps the church did have a new pastor. Maybe, I had changed and how I looked at things had been radically altered.

If this wasn't a miracle enough, the impossible happened. One of our faithful elder board members shared a dream his wife had. She saw in her night vision the reconstructed building with a balcony filled with people. The original plans had called for risers and a balcony, but we had never finished them out. After he shared this dream, our board discussed whether this was the time to install additional seating. There would never be a better time to install them than during the reconstruction. But, the facts said that we shouldn't do it: the insurance company was fighting and discounting the claim; our church's attendance, though growing, did not demand the additional seating; and financially, we weren't sure we could afford it. As we prayed about it, however, a holy boldness came upon that group of men. There was a sense that we couldn't compromise on the dream God had given us. So, we added an additional 400-500 seats to the reconstructed auditorium.

I'm glad we did. What we sensed then was that God was bringing the church back stronger than ever...and He did! The numbers continued to grow until the floor level was two-thirds filled by the time we came back to the building. The news media was there for that first service. Twenty months after the storm, we were back in our building humbler and more thankful than ever.

The church continued to grow. This book will initially be published at the same time that our second phase is completed. The second phase, the "Ministry Center," replaces the square footage lost by the sale of our family life center. The church has doubled since the storm. Not all is rosy. Some five years after the storm, we have still not settled the financial matters with the insurance carrier. Total resolution, however, is not needed to celebrate what God has done.

There are angels in the whirlwinds. God has His way in the storm.

The storm brought many needed changes to our church. We became less confident in surroundings than in the arm of God. He sustained us and saw us through this horrible time.

The microbial growth that had afflicted our church reminded me of the "house leprosy" described in Leviticus. I think over time we can develop attitudes and mindsets that are not pleasing to God. The simple washing with water by the Word of God doesn't cleanse these stains. It takes a prolonged time of stress to bring about the cleansing needed—debilitating sickness, chronic need, or financial stress. Storms provide the radical and remedial treatment needed during such times.

The stress was immense. My right arm throughout this time was my office assistant, Barbara Minton. Our office had been relocated to some space in a strip center next to a Caribbean restaurant. As the aroma of curry, garlic, and pepper wafted through the hastily-erected partitions of our office, I would frequently walk into Barbara's office, plop down in a chair, and together we tried to talk each other from the edge of the cliff. Shortly after we returned to our church, Barbara learned that she suffered from an aggressive form of brain cancer. An emergency surgery took place at the same time we were hosting the 2010 General Conference at the Toyota Center in Houston. The initial prognosis seemed good. Over time, however, the cancer returned and Barbara was taken from us. Her loss devastated her family, our church office, our district and me as well. One of my few confidantes had been taken from me.

It seems that each loss drove me closer to the Lord. God's specialty has always been the impossible. Gargantuan problems call for the great God. Nothing or no one else is capable of filling His shoes.

As our sojourn in the rented facility came to a close, I preached to our church that the risen Christ was seen "in the midst" of the seven golden candlesticks (Revelation 1:12-13). This is His preferred position—in the midst, at the center of it all. I recalled in the message the words penned in the journal of Jim Elliot, the evangelical missionary who perished at the hands of the Auca Indians in Ecuador called the "worst people on Earth" (*TIME Magazine*, "Ecuador: Mission to the Aucas," January 23, 1956). Elliott is most known for the explanation given for his life, "He is no fool who gives what he cannot keep to gain that which he cannot lose." Yet, the words that I chose from his journal were not these, but a prayer offered by Elliott:

86

"Lord, I would re-center my spiritual life as Jacob does in this portion. Instead of Bethel, he centers his experience on El Bethel—not the house of God but the God of that house. Often I feel compassion for Thy Church, because it is visible and can be physically apprehended, but I would not have that be my concern any longer. Lord, I want to be centering my interest on Thee, the God of God's house" (Jim Elliott's journal, January 29, 1948).

> *You may never know that Jesus is all you need, until Jesus is all you have.*
>
> *—Corrie Ten Boom*

Stripped of Bethel, we focused on El-Bethel. Taken from the house of God, we set our gaze on the God of God's house. It was a painful ordeal coming to grips with the fact that we had relied more upon the facility than we had on divinity. God will be found at the center or He will be found nowhere at all.

One of the seemingly less spiritual lessons we learned from the storm was to be proactive. After Hurricane Katrina, our church had become a place of refuge for many people who had fled the New Orleans area. After Ike, our church, damaged though we were, gave to other churches in our area in need. We made mortgage notes, paid for roof repairs, and provided housing for pastors. Yet, there was no one, it seemed, to help us. A few pastors called to encourage me and this was greatly appreciated, but the problems were so immense that no one knew how to help us.

This experience started our creation of a disaster relief coalition. We purposed that mechanisms would be established whereby churches could help one another in times of need. Our churches united to see things happen. After the wildfires that burned hundreds of homes south and west of Austin in 2011, we assisted in getting much needed relief to those people in need. After Hurricane Sandy hit the northeast in 2012, we helped bring hundreds of thousands of dollars of relief to the area. Sometimes, storms awaken us to the needs around us and help us plan accordingly.

The greatest lesson from the storm, however, was to trust in the unseen hand of God. He knows where we are. He also knows the storm will change us if we allow it to do so.

The psalmist said that righteous flourish like the palm tree (Psalm 92:12). I read somewhere that the palm tree can grow up to a foot during a storm. The tree may be lashed and brought to the ground by the storm, but afterwards it stands taller and stronger than ever. Storms are fresh reminders of the Easter message: you may fall, but you shall arise.

SECTION IV

JOSEPH'S THIRD LOW POINT: MEETING BETRAYAL

CHAPTER 11:

EVERYONE HAS A DOTHAN

We have this thing about the number three. We can't decide if we like it or if we dislike it. Contrary adages illustrate this: "The third time is a charm" and "Three strikes and you're out."

Joseph's third low point was the most defining of his life. It's the midway point in the five valleys he faced and it is by far the most challenging of them all. The first two low points were difficult for Joseph, but this one forms the cataclysmic breach between Canaan and Egypt, father and son, and brothers and brother.

Each climber who attempts to summit Mount Everest will have to pass through the Khumbu icefall. This icefall doesn't appear treacherous, but 10 percent of the known deaths on the mountain take place here. This ever-moving, ever-changing glacier is home to frequent icefalls that crush climbers. The greatest danger, however, is the random opening of the ice before the climbers' feet revealing seemingly bottomless crevasses into which climbers simply disappear and are never seen again.

Dothan is the Khumbu icefall of Joseph's life. What happened at Dothan is a study in human nature, sibling rivalry, demonic activity and, oh yes, divine grace. For Dothan is where Joseph became the person God meant Him to be.

It's fitting that Dothan lies midway in these low points. For this reason, we are going to spend more time on this than his other four valleys. We will also do some flash-forwards in his life to show what Joseph learned at Dothan and how Joseph's allegiance and reliance shifted from his earthly father and family to his heavenly Father and to Heaven.

As you read this chapter, remember this important lesson: everyone has a Dothan. You may be entering Dothan or exiting the same. You may be in the midst of Dothan now and be fighting the feelings of betrayal and an unforgiving spirit.

No seasoned climber would cross the Khumbu icefalls without a guide, and no sincere person of faith would tackle life alone. Let the Old Testament picture of Jesus be your guide here. Joseph has something to share with you. Read closely.

Joseph met a "certain man" in Shechem. If indeed this was a theophany, an appearance of God in the Old Testament, then Heaven directed Joseph to the lowest point of his life. One could say that Dothan was God-arranged, ordered by the Lord. Heaven didn't point Joseph to a life of ease and comfort, but to one of severe strain and testing.

It's a forgotten aspect of God: He divides. We focus on the multiplicative aspect of Creation: God multiplied the fish in the sea, the animals on the land, and the fowls in the air. But, we forget before the multiplication, there was division. God divided the firmaments. God separated land from sea, night from darkness, heaven from earth. It can and should be said of God that His great creativity lies in knowing when to divide and when to multiply.

We magnify unity and indeed we should. Unity has a powerful place in Scripture. It's good to dwell together in unity for there the presence of the Lord abides (Psalm 133). The disciples in the upper room were in one mind and one accord prior to the outpouring of the Spirit (Acts 2). Unity is a prelude to Pentecost. The heavenly realm is marked with unity, and we should pray that earth is the mirror image of such unity.

Yet, no great work of God begins without division. God separated Abraham from his people and homeland. He drew fishermen from their nets. Individual salvation begins with a division from the old way of life.

In the biblical days and in certain parts of the world today, the threshing floor was a common sight. Here farmers would winnow the grain separating the wheat from the chaff. Generally the threshing floor was elevated—the highest place around such that the breezes from the distant ocean were felt. As the farmer tossed the grain into the air, the wind did its work of division, separating the lighter chaff from the denser grain.

John the Baptist pointed people to Jesus saying, "He shall baptize you with the Holy Ghost, and with fire." We rejoice in this outpouring, but John did not stop there. He also said that Christ had a fan in His hand and He would thoroughly purge the threshing floor (Matthew 3:11-12). The same Spirit that divided in Creation is dividing the new creation. Old things must pass away before all things can be new.

At Dothan, God separated the wheat from the chaff. He separated Joseph from his brethren. He tore away the dreamer from the hands of the dream-stealers and dream-killers. He separated the dream that the dream might live. Had God not done so, it was obvious that Joseph would be killed.

Yes, God sent Joseph to Dothan. What may have appeared cruel at the time was veiled mercy, grace incognito, and compassion disguised. Through Dothan, God allowed Joseph to become who he was meant to be.

An old rabbinical tale is told of the way of a prophet. Many versions exist of this story with varied elements, but they carry the same message. The story as it was first shared with me involved an elderly prophet doing his work on God's behalf. A young man desired to be the prophet's protégé and to walk in his steps. He pestered the prophet for some time, finally the prophet yielded.

"I will let you walk with me," the prophet told the young man, "under one condition."

"Yes," the young man replied eagerly, "I will promise anything."

Staring deep into the young man's eyes, the prophet said, "Promise me that you will never question anything I say or do."

The young man looked quizzically at the elder prophet and wondered about such an odd statement. Nevertheless he promised and began walking with the prophet.

The first day they traveled some distance late into the afternoon. The sun had almost set when they came upon a small walled city. A small group of men were busy digging a drainage ditch outside the city walls. The prophet greeted the men and asked if one of them could provide him and the young man with a meal and a place to stay for the evening. The ditch diggers jeered and mocked the prophet and told him there would be no food or shelter for him in the city. The prophet and his young traveling companion did not eat that night and slept on the streets.

Early the next morning the prophet and young man left the city. They passed by the ditch where the men were just assembling to work. The prophet lifted his mantle and immediately the ditch was miraculously finished. The workers rejoiced and slapped backs thankful that the task was over and they would be rewarded handsomely for finishing early.

The young man turned to face the prophet and started to ask him why he had finished the ditch for such rude men but he remembered his promise. He had promised to never question the prophet. So, he kept his silence.

They walked the entire day in another direction. The prophet seemed to know where they were going, but the young man was unaware of their destination. At evening they arrived at a modest house where a woman was starting a fire. When she realized the prophet had come to her house, she immediately cooked for him and the young man. That night they ate their fill while the woman and her small son ate nothing. The woman insisted that they sleep inside on the beds and she and her son slept outside on a pile of hay near to her sole prized possession, a milk cow.

Just as the sun was rising, the prophet stirred the young man. They slipped outside of the house and saw the woman and her son still sleeping outside. Standing beside the sleeping pair was the woman's prized cow. The prophet raised his mantle and the cow fell over dead. The prophet and a very confused and distraught young man left without extending their regards and gratitude for the meal and shelter.

Shortly thereafter, the prophet led the young man across a rickety bridge that spanned a deep gorge. Another young man approached from the opposite direction. He greeted the prophet with an outstretched hand and a smile on his face. The prophet said nothing but lifted his mantle and the young man fell from the bridge to his death on the rocks below. The prophet didn't stop to look but just kept walking.

The young man was astonished. When they reached the end of the bridge, he stopped the prophet.

"I know I promised I would never ask you why you do what you do, but I must break that promise. I must know why you were kind to the ditch diggers who were mean to us. I must know why you killed the cow of the woman who was nice to us. I have to know why you apparently killed a man who did nothing to us."

The prophet gazed silently for a few moments at the young man. Finally, he spoke.

"This one time I will try to answer your questions," said the prophet. "The ditch diggers were within feet of striking gold and would have fortunes beyond their imaginations. Because they were not open to the ways of God, they will now work for the rest of their lives."

The young man nodded and asked, "What about the cow?"

"While you slept last night, I was awake," the prophet said. "The woman's son was supposed to die, but I convinced the death angel to take the cow instead."

The young man said nothing while the prophet continued.

"And the young man who just fell off of the gorge was journeying to a distant country where he would lose his testimony and walk with God. His mother was praying that God would not let him die lost." The prophet paused and said quietly, "He didn't die lost."

The young man covered his face with his hands and began to weep. The prophet then said, "Never question the way of a prophet. For the way of a prophet is the way of God."

A fanciful and somewhat dreadful story, but it demonstrates the truth found in God's world: His ways are beyond our understanding. When we can't track Him, we must trust Him.

Joseph trusted the "certain man" at Shechem. He journeyed a few more miles until he came to Dothan. He must have seen his brothers and his father's flock in the distance, but he was unaware of what his brethren were saying and doing as he approached.

Let's walk through the conversation and actions of Joseph's brethren at Dothan.

We first read, "they conspired against him to slay him" (Genesis 37:18). Here we see the animosity of the visionless majority against the dreaming minority, against those who can dream. Those who see less despise people who see more.

The natural enemy of the mighty eagle is the condor. The eagle soars high, sees far and feeds on fresh kills. The condor is a scavenger that feeds on dead things. As with the eagle, people of faith are constantly challenged by those who are addicted to low living and feasting on the dead things of this world. The condor's advantage to the soaring eagle is found in its weight. If the condor can grasp the soaring eagle in its claws it will simply quit flying and plummet to the earth bringing the eagle down with him. That's what the enemy longs to do: bring us down.

The hatred possessed by Joseph's brethren was deep. It can be sensed in what they said to one another, "Behold, this dreamer cometh" (Genesis 37:19). They didn't call Joseph by his name, rather they called him "our brother" (37:26, 27), "the child" (37:30) and to Jacob, "thy son" (37:32). To say the name of Joseph is to repeat the prayer of Rachel, "May he increase." And Joseph's brethren did not want Joseph to increase, but to decrease.

Scripture tells us of their evil plan: "Come now therefore, and let us slay him, and cast him into some pit, and we will say, Some evil beast hath devoured him: and we shall see what will become of his dreams" (Genesis 37:20).

In Scott Peck's *People of the Lie*, he described a phenomenon called "group evil." He hypothesized that people can be worse together than they are separately. Each of Joseph's ten older brothers despised their younger brother, but together they did something that probably any one of them would not have done by himself: they conspired to kill their younger brother.

Fratricide is an old sin. The world's first murder was Cain slaying his brother. This sounds so foreign to our ears. We believe that blood is thicker than water and that a brother is born for adversity. When the going gets tough, those nearest and dearest to us will stand with us in a family-right-or-wrong devotion. Yet, this isn't always the case. To put it more plainly, sometimes those nearest to us hurt us the most.

Junius Brutus Booth was a world-renowned Shakespearean actor who fled to America after having a tryst with a young Londoner named Mary. Two of their sons, Edwin and John, vied for their father's thespian mantle. Edwin had the looks, the voice, and the native talent to excel. John had no mentors and struggled on stage, but he was athletic and could perform stunts that others couldn't. Edwin's rising star soon eclipsed that of his brother, John, and he became America's most famous actor. He performed the lead role in *Hamlet* for one hundred straight nights before packed houses in his Winter Garden Theater in New York City. Edwin performed in *Hamlet* in Washington, DC, by request of President Lincoln. Edwin's fame waxed larger; John's fame waned smaller.

In her historical work, *My Thoughts Be Bloody,* Nora Titone traces this sibling rivalry against the larger backdrop of fratricide known as the Civil War. Edwin sided with the North; John with the South. John's leap from the balcony of Ford's Theater—typical theatrical tradecraft for John Wilkes Booth—was perhaps simply another effort to outperform his brother.

Edwin Booth may have been more famous, but John Wilkes Booth was more infamous. Edwin may have had the affection of his late father, but John slew the well-loved Father Abe. Jealous brethren act with this mindset: if I can't have it, I will kill someone or something.

"Jealousy," Solomon once said, "is cruel as the grave" (Song of Solomon 8:6). But, when jealousy and betrayal are witnessed amongst brethren, they are at their cruelest.

Joseph's older brothers went through three renditions of how to hurt Joseph. They first thought to kill him and throw his body into a pit (Genesis 37:18-20). Reuben suggested a modification of the plan saying, in effect, "Let's skip the killing part. Just throw him into the pit" (37:22). So, the brothers tore the coat of many colors from Joseph's shoulders and threw him into the pit. Reuben, it seemed, planned to double back and help Joseph escape the pit when his brothers' attention was elsewhere (37:29-30). But, while Reuben was gone, an Ishmaelite caravan bound for Egypt passed by. Judah offered the final plan, "Let's not kill him. Let's not leave him in the pit. Let's sell him to these guys!" (37:26-28).

Thirty pieces of silver was the going price for a slave (Exodus 21:32; Matthew 26:15). So low was his brethren's opinion of Joseph, they betrayed him for a bargain price: twenty pieces of silver.

Yes, there is no cruelty like that from within. David spoke of something similar. Ahithophel had been David's most trusted and reliable advisor, but this elder turned his back on David. David's hurt made its way into a song: "It was not an enemy that reproached me; then I could have borne it: neither was it he that hated me that did magnify himself against me; then I would have hid myself from him: But it was thou, a man mine equal, my guide, and mine acquaintance. We took sweet counsel together, and walked unto the house of God in company" (Psalm 55:12-14).

The greatest betrayal can be born from the sweetest fellowship. You don't have to take my word for that, you can ask God about it. He will tell you it is so. After all, the same thing happened to Him. Lucifer was the anointed cherub. His position in the heavenly realm was undisputed, but his pride led to his betrayal of the Lord.

Jesus had eleven loyal disciples, but one betrayed him. Jesus called Judas his friend, but that didn't stop Judas from selling Jesus out for thirty pieces of silver.

I think you get the picture. If it happened to Joseph and Jesus, it will happen to you. Those in whom you trust will shatter your confidence in them. Loved ones will let you down and will hurt you the most.

That's what Dothan is all about: jealousy and betrayal. If you haven't been there, you will be. If you're there now, there's hope.

We know there was a deep, cruel pit in this place, but Dothan also means the "place of two wells." No matter how deep the pit, there are always refreshing fountains from which to draw.

CHAPTER 12:

DRINKING FROM TWIN FOUNTAINS

My pastor used a favorite saying when he advised someone on how to handle life's seeming unfairness. "Always," he would say to his congregation, "keep a right spirit." This five-word sentence is easier said than done. Life sometimes throws hard blows against us and we don't always respond with a right spirit.

God did not make us like crustaceans with exoskeletons that can withstand both direct and glancing blows. He made us with an endoskeleton, meaning that the tough stuff is covered by the soft stuff. It also means we can be hurt and wounded. God made us to feel injustice, not to repel it.

Dothan is found in Genesis 37 and if our attention were focused solely on that chapter, we would never know how Joseph felt during this time. Thankfully, the rest of the story is given later in Genesis.

Let's fast-forward fifteen years and beyond two additional low points in Joseph's life. He is now second in command over all of Egypt. Famine gripped Egypt and extended its bony fingers into Canaan. Joseph foresaw the famine and prepared a vast supply to see his people through the lean times. Based on nothing more than a rumor, Jacob sends the same ten brothers who had thrown Joseph into the pit to Egypt to buy grain.

Providence arranged that the once-defenseless Joseph would then have all the power when he encountered his brothers again. They bowed before this stranger governor and Joseph remembered the dream he had in his innocent years—the dream his brethren despised so much (Genesis 42:6-9). Joseph knew his brethren, but they did not know him.

Joseph had to decide what to do with them. Could he trust them? Should he? Why even take the risk? Joseph risked it for a variety of reasons. Only they had some answers that he needed so desperately—whether his father and younger brother, Benjamin, were alive and how they were fairing. More than this, Joseph wanted to see if they had truly changed.

He put his ten older brothers through a series of tests. They may seem complicated and somewhat meaningless to us, yet they were designed to reveal if his brethren were trustworthy. He speaks roughly to them and accuses them of being spies. They responded, "Thy servants are twelve brethren, the sons of one man in the land of Canaan; and, behold, the youngest is this day with our father, and one is not" (Genesis 42:13).

Joseph gleaned much information from his brethren's response. First, they still counted him in their number: they were "twelve brethren." He also learned that his father, Jacob, was alive and that his father had kept Benjamin from making the trip with these ten brothers. Joseph must have assumed that his father Jacob blamed these ten boys for the loss of Joseph and would not trust Benjamin to them. The ten men had said that Joseph "is not," but Joseph chose not to challenge them but to test them instead.

"You are spies," said Joseph to his brethren through an interpreter. "By the life of Pharaoh," Joseph continued, "you will not leave this place until your younger brother comes here."

Joseph pondered that perhaps one of them would be allowed to go home and fetch Benjamin. He then commanded all ten to be thrown into prison, a place with which he was all too familiar. Joseph's ten brothers remained in prison for three days and were then returned to him.

The brothers now witnessed a much kinder and gentler Egyptian governor. He told them that he feared God and would permit nine of the brothers to return home with food for their families. One brother, however, would remain in captivity until Benjamin was returned to Egypt. This would prove to Joseph that they were "true men."

The thought of facing their father, Jacob, with one brother left behind was difficult enough. It was too fresh an experience with them and they never wanted to revisit that pain again. To tell Jacob that the brothers all had to return to Egypt with his youngest son, Benjamin, to gain the release of another son to appease this strange governor pushed these men over the edge.

Forgetting where they stood, the brethren began talking amongst themselves. In this Egyptian palace, Joseph heard the words that he had longed to hear. His brothers were sorry for what they had done.

"They said one to another, We are verily guilty concerning our brother, in that we saw the anguish of his soul, when he besought us, and we would not hear; therefore is this distress come upon us. And Reuben answered them, saying, Spake I not unto you, saying, Do not sin against the child; and ye would not hear?" therefore, behold, also his blood is required" (Genesis 42:21-22).

Joseph's brothers did not know this strange governor understood what they said, but when Joseph heard these candid and heartfelt words, the feelings in his own heart overwhelmed him.

"My brothers do feel sorry for what they have done," Joseph must have thought. "Even today they can still hear my cries from that pit in

Dothan. They are not as cold and ruthless as I imagined. They feel my anguish and remember my pain to this day."

"I thought I knew them," Joseph may have reasoned to himself, "but maybe I don't know them anymore than they know me. Perhaps, they've changed. They've admitted their guilt. They've acknowledged their sin."

Joseph lost his composure, which would not do, of course, since he was not supposed to understand these men. He turned away from the men and walked away. His brethren were so lost in their discussions that they didn't notice Joseph's absence. Nor did they see his trembling shoulders or hear him weeping in the shadows.

Dothan is the place of two wells. To this day, one can take the trip to see these wells. One has a shrine built above it and is recognized as the pit in which Joseph was thrown.

In a very real sense, there are two abiding fountains found in the low point of betrayal. The fountains sustained Joseph for fifteen years. Anyone who has been betrayed should never stray too far from these fountains for without them he will perish.

The first refreshing fountain suggested by Dothan is this: People do change. The person who hurt you years ago is not the same person today. When you hold to the hurt you experienced, you're holding to a mug shot of the offender from a day gone by.

Ask yourself this question, "Are you the same person

> *Time heals griefs and quarrels, for we change and are no longer the same persons. Neither the offender nor the offended are any more themselves.*
>
> *—Blaise Pascal*

104

you were back then?" Aren't you wiser, kinder, more thoughtful, more loyal, less judgmental, and more forgiving? Then is it too much of a stretch to think that the people who once hurt you have learned from their mistakes, paid for them dearly, and are no longer the same people they once were?

It's been many years since I graduated from high school. On occasion, however, I will run into a former classmate. After the awkward remembering of each other's names and former faces, the conversation invariably turns back to the past. Unless there is a current relationship, all we have to remember is the past.

Few of us will have a similar opportunity as Joseph to hear the people who hurt us come face to face with their guilt and shame. So when we can't take someone at face value, we should accept them at "faith value," believing the best and the noblest about the person who wronged us.

Such behavior is called Christianity.

Before we were called Christians (Acts 11:26), we were called people of "the way" (Acts 9:2). Christianity is based on a Person, the One who called Himself the Way (John 14:6). Our faith is less a codified collection of doctrine as it is a way of life. And the Christian way of life is dissimilar to all other ways.

Jesus forgave people even as they crucified Him. He was the Sheep who didn't open His mouth to the accusers (Isaiah 53:7). He allowed Judas to get close enough to kiss His cheek and in that act of betrayal, Jesus still called him friend. God is love and Love Incarnate believed all things, hoped all things, and endured all things (I Corinthians 13:7).

Jesus modeled the way we should live. On that day when the religious mob threatened to stone a woman caught in the act of adultery, Jesus advised them that only the one without sin should cast

105

the first stone. The only sinless One in the midst was writing in sand, not clinging to sharp, jagged rocks. His way was open-handed, not close-fisted.

Notice the crowd's response that day. "And they which heard it, being convicted by their own conscience, went out one by one, beginning at the eldest, even unto the last: and Jesus was left alone, and the woman standing in the midst" (John 8:9).

Each accuser was convicted not only by the voice of Jesus, but also by the voice of his own conscience. Notice the order of the departure: from the eldest to the youngest. The older they were, the more understanding they were of the frailties of mankind. This could be called the lesson of longevity.

It's not recorded that any of these people stopped and apologized to the woman for their treatment of her. They simply left and she found herself alone in the presence of Jesus.

May each betrayed person find himself or herself in a similar place! For only Jesus truly comprehends the depth and the breadth of your hurt. He too was wounded in the house of His friends (Zechariah 13:6). He who knew no sin was pierced and wounded for the sins of others. Roman soldiers may have crucified Him, but only at the request of His brethren. Betrayal bites deeper than the lash, the nail, and the thorn.

After the Resurrection, Jesus still bore the scars but you don't read that Jesus talked much about the denials and the betrayals. He focused more on the future and less on the past.

We struggle with this. We cling to past hurts and disappointments and God help the person who tries to pry them from our grasp. Our fallen human nature focuses on those poor souls who crossed our path and seemed determined to destroy or damage us.

Stephen Crane is best known for his seminal work, *The Red Badge of Courage*, but he also penned other works. A poem called, "In the Desert," speaks to me:

> *In the desert*
> *I saw a creature, naked, bestial,*
> *Who, squatting upon the ground,*
> *Held his heart in his hands,*
> *And ate of it.*
> *I said, "Is it good, friend?"*
> *"It is bitter—bitter," he answered;*
> *"But I like it*
> *Because it is bitter,*
> *And because it is my heart."*

Crane suggests that folks who hold bitterness in their hearts are animalistic, not divine; squatting, not standing; alone, not in the company of others. This is not a pretty picture of bitterness, is it? Yet, there's some truth here.

Someone once said that success is 10 percent what happens to us and 90 percent how we respond to it. Our response to the injustices and injuries that come our way can range from self-pity to revenge, but somewhere in this range of responses, a door should be propped open in our spirit permitting Heaven to enter.

Give God a chance to work with people who've hurt you. Give Him a chance to change them. The same God who works on you will work on them as well.

One of my favorite quotes from John Maxwell involves the possibility of change. Maxwell said, "People change when they hurt enough that they have to, learn enough that they want to, or receive enough that they are able to." People do change once they hurt enough, learn enough, or receive enough. Until the brim of "enough" is reached, change will not take place. Faith gives God time to bring the needed change.

For twenty years—the interval of time between Joseph's last encounter with his brethren in Dothan—we read nothing in Scripture of Joseph plotting and scheming revenge against those who had hurt him. We search in vain for a verse in Scripture that Joseph even focused on his hurt at all. Surely, he must have recalled it at times. Maybe the hurt swept over him periodically like waves. Perhaps he had to pray hard and long to keep this bitterness from lodging in his spirit.

It's also worthy to note that with such hurt, Joseph did not have a relationship with those who hurt him. There is no record of correspondences. Joseph was second in command of Egypt and could have easily dispatched a courier to check on his family and his father, but he did not. This suggests Joseph understood something very profound: if there were to be any change on his brethren's part, it would not come from him, but only from God. He took his hands off of the situation. He turned it over to God.

We are fixers by nature. The problem, to our way of thinking, was that we didn't

> *For you who wonder if you've played too long to change, take courage from Jacob's legacy. No man is too bad for God. To transform a riverboat gambler into a man of faith would be no easy task. But for God, it was all in a night's work.*
>
> *—Max Lucado*

communicate enough, spend time enough, and give enough. We compensate for our perceived failures by talking more, spending more time, giving more of ourselves. The situation rarely changes, however, because people haven't changed. And people only change when they hurt enough, learn enough, and receive enough.

The God who is enough is the only One who can truly bring lasting change. We repair; He restores. We reform; He transforms.

Until God brings the change, we drink deep from that first well of Dothan—people can change. But, we can't change them. Only God can. Put it in His hands and leave it there.

A heavenly timer eventually sounded and God said, "Enough." Joseph's servants tell him of ten men who claimed to be brothers from Canaan wanting to buy food.

"Could it be?" Joseph must have wondered. "What are the chances of this happening?"

If you give God time, the chances are actually very high that resolution and reconciliation will take place. The day may come when you hear those who hurt you pour out their confessions before you. You, like Joseph, will then understand how bad they've suffered all these many years.

Joseph's brother Simeon was placed in bonds and carried away from the others. Joseph commanded his servants to fill his brother's sacks with grain and to place their silver in the bags as well. The nine brothers take their leave.

Upon their return to Canaan they rehearse the events with the strange governor to their father. They tell him that to rescue Simeon from prison, they must return with Benjamin. Jacob refuses to hear of it. "Joseph is not, and Simeon is not, and ye will take Benjamin away: all these things are against me" (Genesis 42:36).

The brothers emptied their sacks of the grain and the silver used to purchase the grain spilled out as well. Fear gripped the entire family. Not only would the governor accuse them of being spies, he would now accuse them of being thieves.

The grain ran out. Jacob told his sons to go buy more grain. His sons reminded him that the Egyptian governor would require Benjamin to be brought with them. Judah pledged to his father that he would return with Benjamin and only then did Jacob reluctantly allow them to go. Jacob sent gifts to the governor and instructed his sons to take double money with them. They returned to Egypt with Benjamin.

The brothers tried to return the silver found in their sacks on the previous journey. Joseph refused it saying that God had blessed them. He brought Simeon from prison and for the first time in twenty years, all twelve brothers were together.

They presented their father's gift to Joseph and Joseph's heart was touched. "Is your father well? Is he yet alive?" (Genesis 43:27). When Joseph saw his brother Benjamin, his only full brother, he again lost his composure and had to leave the room to weep for a while.

But Joseph had to know his brethren's hearts. He had a banquet prepared for his brothers. He instructed his servants to place five times as much food before Benjamin as the other brothers. No doubt Joseph was watching his older brothers' reaction to the younger brother receiving more.

Satisfied with their response, a final test remained. He instructed his servants to not only fill his brothers' sacks with grain and the silver with which they had purchased the grain, but Joseph also commanded that his personal silver cup be placed in Benjamin's sack.

His brothers then took their leave. Happy and satisfied, they journeyed toward Canaan. They hadn't made much progress when Joseph's steward overtook them. He demanded to know why they had mistreated his master by stealing his silver cup. The brothers denied stealing the cup and said that should this cup be found amongst one of them, that person would be Joseph's slave.

As their cargo was searched, Joseph's brothers must have grown apprehensive when they saw the silver purchase price in the top of each sack of grain. The steward started with the eldest and worked to the youngest until he found the cup in Benjamin's sack.

The steward must have seized Benjamin. The brothers began tearing their clothes and crying out. Quickly they returned to Joseph's house and fell before him. They offered themselves to be Joseph's slaves. Joseph instructed all of them but Benjamin to return to their father.

Judah had made a pledge to his father and lived up to it. He stepped forward and spoke from his heart that they couldn't return to Jacob without Benjamin. He told Joseph of what Jacob said before they left, that he had two sons from Rachel. One was torn to pieces and he has not seen him since. And if this second son from Rachel were taken from him, Jacob would die. Judah then offers himself up as Joseph's slave so long as Benjamin could go home.

Joseph now realized his brothers had passed the test. They had truly

> *Nothing paralyzes our lives like the attitude that things can never change. We need to remind ourselves that God can change things. Outlook determines outcome. If we see only the problems, we will be defeated; but if we see the possibilities in the problems, we can have victory.*
>
> *—Warren Wiersbe*

changed. He could refrain himself no longer. He commanded his servants to leave the room. Then, Joseph surprised these eleven men from Canaan by speaking in their language. But, they quickly got over the surprise of him speaking in their language when he said: "I am Joseph your brother, whom ye sold into Egypt" (Genesis 45:4).

Joseph started crying. His crying was so loud that the house of Pharaoh heard his sorrowful sobs. Inner fountains had burst forth inside of Joseph, refusing to be tamed. Long years of wondering, hoping, and believing had come to this place and he could not be silent any longer.

The second fountain that had seen Joseph through since Dothan was then revealed. He told his brethren that there was a famine that would last another five years in the land. Had Joseph not been sent to Egypt, his family would not have survived. He makes some profound statements to his brothers.

- "Be not grieved, nor angry with yourselves, that ye sold me hither: for God did send me before you to preserve life" (Genesis 45:5).

- "God sent me before you to preserve you a posterity in the earth, and to save your lives by a great deliverance. So now it was not you that sent me hither, but God" (Genesis 45:7-8).

The second fountain is the knowledge that God uses all things to accomplish His purpose in our lives. God is in control. Like Joseph, we should drink deep from that knowledge.

Joseph's story is largely confined to the Book of Genesis, but there is an interesting statement made of him at the opening of the Book of Exodus. Moses started this book by listing the names of the eleven brothers who came into Egypt with their father Jacob. "And all the souls that came out of the loins of Jacob were seventy souls,"

Moses wrote. But, then, inspired by the Spirit he added this phrase, "For Joseph was in Egypt already" (Exodus 1:5).

Everything that happened to Joseph was to put him in position to be used by God. Before Jacob saw the famine, Joseph saw it coming. God positioned Joseph at the right arm of Pharaoh to save not only Egypt but also to save Israel.

Methodist founder John Wesley used the expression "prevenient grace." A more modern expression would be "preceding grace" or the grace that goes before. Wesley used the expression to describe God's grace that touches fallen man permitting him to respond in faith to God.

I want to use this phrase to describe this second well of Dothan. God's grace goes before us much as Joseph went before Israel. God knows tomorrow and permits difficulties in our present to prepare us for miracles in our future.

Joseph was in Egypt already. That was the revelation that came to Joseph when he watched his eleven brothers kneeling before him. He had been sent on ahead. God allowed his brothers to strip his favored robe from his shoulders. And was it any accident that an Ishmaelite band passed by journeying to Egypt? No, God was positioning Joseph to be in the place He needed for him to be.

Do we really believe that God is at work in our lives? That He takes the good and the bad, the consequential and inconsequential, the high points and low points and uses them all to accomplish His purpose?

Our days pass like a weaver's shuttle. Time is a thread and choices give the thread color and texture. And God weaves all things into a majestic and intricate tapestry of His own design. Benjamin Malachi Franklin (1882-1965) expressed it well in his poem, "The Weaver."

My life is but a weaving
between my Lord and me;
I cannot choose the colors
He worketh steadily.

Oft times He weaveth sorrow
And I, in foolish pride,
Forget He sees the upper,
And I the underside.

Not til the loom is silent
And the shuttles cease to fly,
Shall God unroll the canvas
And explain the reason why.

The dark threads are as needful
In the Weaver's skillful hand,
As the threads of gold and silver
In the pattern He has planned.

Jacob had fashioned a coat of many colors, but the heavenly Father fashions one that is beyond our understanding. Where we see chaos, He sees order. Where we see knots and confusion, He sees future crowns. He fashions all things in our lives according to His purpose.

Solomon said that we lead our lives "under the sun" and we cannot gain a glimpse of what God sees. We see things from our limited perspective. We focus on the hurts, the misunderstandings, and the disappointments. But, God sees how these low points helped define us and prepare us for the days ahead.

This second fountain of Dothan is crucial for God's will to be done. Joseph had to believe not only that people could change, but also that God knew what He was doing. He couldn't live as a victim of the past; he had to claim the promises of the future. Not only did his future depend on this, but also the future of all of Israel.

This deepest low point in Joseph's life happened in the place of two wells. Life's pits come equipped with wells. If you're in a low point and look carefully enough, you will find a fountain to sustain you.

For a special video from the author with additional information, please visit the following:

http://thepointoflowpoints.wordaflamepress.com/lpsection4

DISCUSSION QUESTIONS

SECTION IV: Meeting Betrayal

Chapters 11-12

Discuss the following questions:

1. What feelings do you commonly experience when someone has betrayed you?

2. How do you practice forgiveness of those who have hurt you even when you are still hurt by their actions?

3. The author compared the first of two wells in Dothan to the idea that people—even those who hurt you—do change with God's help. Do you find it difficult to believe that people who hurt you really can change? Like Joseph, must they prove themselves to you before you believe they have changed?

4. The author compared the second well of Dothan to the idea that God works all things for good. Discuss how betrayal can work for good in a person's life.

5. The fanciful story, "The Way of the Prophet," describes the mysterious ways of God. How has God taken betrayals or other hurts in your life and used them to change you?

SECTION V

JOSEPH'S FOURTH LOW POINT: COMBATTING UNJUST ACCUSATIONS

CHAPTER 13:

BEWARE, THE WHISPERER

The fourth low point in Joseph's life is perhaps the most familiar to us, the false accusations raised against him by Potiphar's wife. Its familiarity, however, sometimes causes us to lose sight of its relevance to our daily lives. Not all will lose a parent as a child or will be threatened with murder by jealous brothers, but all of us will at some point in our lives be unjustly accused.

Satan is the accuser of all things righteous. He first appears to Adam and Eve as a serpent in the Garden making unjust accusations against God. It's of interest that one of the Hebrew words for a serpent is *nachash* which is related to the word *nahash* meaning to hiss or to whisper. Satan is the whisperer who is the father of all lies and all whispered and shouted unjust accusations.

Each of the low points in Joseph's life can, in some way, be viewed as satanic in origin. Rachel dies: Satan is the murderer from the beginning (John 8:44). Joseph staggers and wanders: Satan confuses and blinds (II Corinthians 4:4). His brethren seek to destroy Joseph's dream: Satan is the destroyer (Revelation 9:11). But, never is Satan's power more clearly and commonly seen than in his ability to hurl false accusations at the righteous (Revelation 12:10).

Prolific author Warren Wiersbe wrote a small, but excellent book many years ago entitled *The Strategy of Satan*. In the book, he speaks of how the enemy of our soul attacks the righteous:

- As deceiver, Satan targets our mind. His weapons are lies. Our defense is the Word of God. "It is written..."
- As destroyer, Satan attacks our body. He uses suffering and seeks to make us impatient with God's will. Our defense is the sustaining grace of God.
- As ruler, Satan seeks to subvert our will from God's will. His chief weapon in this area is our own pride. Our defense is the indwelling, empowering Spirit of God.
- As accuser, Satan attacks our "inner man," our heart and conscience. His weapon is accusation and his intent is to destroy our credibility before God and man. Our defense is in knowing that Christ withstood these temptations and His example and His intercession for us can sustain us.

None of us is exempt from being attacked by the enemy in all of the above areas, but one of the most hurtful and painful is a Hell-inspired, diabolical, whispering campaign. Joseph was not immune to it, but he shows us how to move through such a low point in life and to cling to our good standing with God and man. Let's walk through this valley with him.

Joseph did not come to Egypt in style; rather, he came bound hand and foot as a slave. A person's entrance matters less than his exit. Jesus entered this world bound hand in foot in the limitations of flesh and because of hatred ended up in Egypt as well. Yet, Christ's exit from this world was marked by ascension into glory. Joseph, the "Jesus of the Old Testament," had a similar radical change of circumstances between his entrance and exit. He would rise from his status as a slave to be the governor of Egypt, second only in power and influence to Pharaoh.

Joseph's journey to Egypt was an unwilling one. The Ishmaelite or Midianite caravan carried the seventeen-year-old Joseph roughly three hundred miles from the pit in Dothan to Egypt, a journey of two to three weeks.

> *The enemy utilizes this desire of keeping the conscience void of offense by accusing us of various things. In mistaking such accusations as being from our own consciences we often lose our peace, tire of trying to keep pace with false accusations, and thus cease to advance spiritually with confidence.*
>
> *—Watchman Nee*

Joseph had a lot of time to think and to ponder his situation. If there were a time for self-pity and despair, this would have been it. However, Scripture is silent on Joseph's thoughts and feelings during this journey. Based on Joseph's attitude and actions as this part of his story unfolds in Genesis 39, the young dreamer must have come to grips with the fact that God was in all of this. He was as ready as he could be for the days ahead.

Joseph entered Egypt and was probably amazed by the crowds, the monuments, and the many languages. His first task was probably to learn a new language. As a Semitic language, ancient Egyptian had some similarities to Hebrew, but for Joseph it was probably a challenge and would require much effort on his part.

Unlike Moses several centuries later, Joseph was not educated in the finest schools of Egypt. Whatever knowledge he possessed was probably parochial and confined mostly in application to the fields of Canaan. Another strike against Joseph was the inconvenient fact that shepherds were abominations to Egyptians (Genesis 46:34). Joseph seemed to have little to offer the most advanced civilization of his day.

Yet he caught the eye of Potiphar, captain of Pharaoh's guard. Joseph was on the auction block and this powerful official saw something in him. Even in chains dreamers stand out in any crowd. Something about his bearing, his confidence, his poise intrigued Potiphar and he purchased Joseph. The negotiated price is not stated, but Potiphar soon realized that Joseph was a blessed man. Joseph returned home with Potiphar and lived in his master's house. Potiphar realized that God was with Joseph and God blessed anything Joseph touched. Joseph was soon put over the household and over all of Potiphar's possessions.

There is a certain buoyancy to blessed people. Their rising tide lifts all around them. The shackles of slavery could not keep Joseph bound. God favored him and it showed. He was blessed in the field and in the city; blessed back in Canaan and now blessed in Egypt. As with his grandfather Abraham, Joseph was blessed to be a blessing (Genesis 12:2). Whatever Joseph touched in Potiphar's house, God blessed: "The Lord blessed the Egyptian's house for Joseph's sake; and the blessing of the Lord was upon all that he had in the house, and in the field" (39:5).

Consider this pattern in Joseph's life. His presence blessed Potiphar. When this chapter of his life ends, we find Joseph in prison. The same thing happens here. The prison-keeper turns over everything to Joseph and again everything Joseph touches begins to prosper because God was with him (39:23). Eventually, when Joseph became governor, the same thing can be said of Pharaoh and all of Egypt.

The blessed person is easily recognized. Blessed people bless people. The common denominator of the blessings on Potiphar's house, the prison, and the seven years of plenty in Egypt was a blessed person: Joseph. And behind Joseph was the abiding, empowering presence of God. Joseph was blessed of God and it showed.

Human wisdom says that all good things must come to an end. With Joseph, we sense the other shoe is about to drop. Potiphar's wife temporarily halted Joseph's upward trajectory by soliciting his attention and sexual favors. Joseph was well built and handsome and he soon caught the eye of Potiphar's wife. She propositioned Joseph, but he refused her.

Joseph to this point has been a man of few words. Outside of his boyish dreams, there is precious little dialogue found in these early years of his life. In this awkward circumstance, Joseph spoke and revealed much of his character and what he valued. He argued that Potiphar has been good to him and trusted him with all that he had— all except his wife. "How then can I do this great wickedness," Joseph queried, "and sin against God?" (Genesis 39:9).

Joseph viewed his life and position as one of trust. Potiphar had shown great trust in him by elevating him and showing him favor. Joseph attempted to reason with Potiphar's wife arguing that he could not violate her husband's trust. More importantly he looked through his human master to the divine and argued further that he could not sin against God.

Several hundred years before God gave Moses the Law, God had already written the seventh commandment against adultery in the heart of Joseph. Joseph was not only a blessed person, but he was also righteous. He understood the character and nature of God and sought to replicate it in his own life. Godliness is a "Yes" and a "No." It's submitting to God and resisting the enemy (James 4:7). The same God-given grace, which enables us to yield to God, causes us to refuse the devil's lies and temptations (Titus 2:11-12). Joseph knew in his heart that to whom much is given, much is required. He had been given much and his behavior had to reflect such.

Daily the tempter came to Joseph; daily he resisted. The final temptation and refusal came when Joseph unwittingly went into his master's house only to discover that he was alone with Potiphar's wife. She took hold of his garment, but he shed his coat and ran from the house.

Joseph had a propensity to change from one garment to the next. In fact, these garments seem to form some natural divisions in his life: the shredded coat of many colors, the abandoned coat in Potiphar's house, and the coat placed on his shoulders by Pharaoh. People who seek to please God are often changing their coats, moving from one phase of their life to another as God slowly peels away what once was to make room for what will be. This may sound romantic or sentimental, but shedding one's coat is painful, vulnerable business.

Potiphar's wife turned from temptress to accuser. Standing with Joseph's coat in her hand and probably infuriated by his refusal of her advances, she did what the whisperer has done for many years: she spread lies. She called for the men of the house because the sower of unjust accusations always demands an audience. Potiphar's wife spun a tale of how Joseph tried to attack her but she resisted him. By the time Potiphar arrived home, she had grown proficient at telling her tale. Her phrases were polished, her timing was impeccable, and righteous indignation poured from her every gesture. Potiphar did what most hearers of lies have done for years: he believed the lie and he acted before he thought.

"The most outrageous lies that can be invented will find believers," Mark Twain once said, "if a man only tells them with all his might." Potiphar's wife turned in an Academy Award winning performance and told the lie with all of her might. Joseph, the favored and blessed man of God, didn't stand a chance. The jury was rigged against him. He was tried and found guilty. Like Jesus before His false accusers, Joseph remained silent. No defense was offered; no explanation was sought.

Satan has a means to at least momentarily stop the forward progress of God. All he needs is a fellow whisperer. In Joseph's case, Potiphar's wife sang in a demonic duet with the whisperer and checked his upward ascent.

Before we go forward with Joseph's low point of unjust accusations, let's look at the father of lies some more. He's called the "accuser of our brethren" (Revelation 12:7-12). Day and night, Satan accuses God's people before God's throne. Pretty brazen, isn't it? In the opening book of the Bible, Satan is accusing God; in the closing book of the Bible, he's accusing God's people. "The holiness of God," said Stephen Charnock in his class work

> *Even doubtful accusations leave a stain behind them.*
>
> —*Thomas Fuller*

The Existence and Attributes of God, "is his glory and crown." Satan's character is likewise crowned with unholy accusations. His kingdom is one of lies and falsehoods.

In Zechariah 3, we see the accuser at work. We are taken into the heavenly realm and we see a high priest named Joshua standing before God. Satan is also there doing what he does best, accusing and resisting this man of God. That he has made headway is revealed by Joshua's dress. Gone are his white robes of righteousness and in their place are filthy garments.

This is where Satan gets his thrills—seeing the once godly reduced from the heavenly realm back to the dust from which he came. Heaven however has a different future for Joshua. The filthy garments and his iniquity are removed. He is restored in garments of white. The competing agendas of Heaven and Hell are clearly seen here: the former exalts; the latter abases.

Another example can be seen in the life of Simon Peter on the eve of Christ's passion. On that fateful night, Judas Iscariot betrayed Jesus and was driven by the destroyer to kill himself. Simon Peter denied Jesus on that same night and wept bitterly. One found repentance. Do you remember what Jesus had told Simon Peter earlier that evening? "Simon, Simon," Jesus said, "Behold, Satan hath desired to have you, that he may sift you as wheat" (Luke 22:31). Satan wanted to grind Simon Peter to powder through guilt and condemnation—those lies we tell ourselves—but Jesus prayed that His chief apostle's faith would survive the test. Again, Heaven seeks to sustain us; Hell seeks to destroy us.

The accuser's weapons of choice are false accusations:

- "You're not good enough."
- "You've failed God in the past."
- "You're not living the life you should."
- "You're not reading the Bible and praying like you should."
- "You're a hypocrite."

In his book *By Grace Alone*, Sinclair Ferguson lists the four major "fiery darts" of Satan against believers:

- Fiery Dart 1: "God is against you," Satan says. "He is not really for you. How can you believe He is for you when you see the things that are happening in your life?"
- Fiery Dart 2: "I have accusations I will bring against you because of your sins," Satan argues. "What can you say in defense? Nothing."
- Fiery Dart 3: "You can say you are forgiven, but there is a payback day coming—a condemnation day," Satan insinuates. "How will you defend yourself then?"
- Fiery Dart 4: "Given your track record, what hope is there that you will persevere to the end?" Satan asks.

We desperately need a shield of faith to defend us from such incendiaries!

Not only does the enemy hurl accusations at you, but he also inspires other to act in his stead. The whisperer begets whisperers and soon the false accusation factory is churning out one lie after another. "A froward [perverse] man soweth strife," said Solomon, "and a whisperer separateth chief friends" (Proverbs 16:28). Whisperers bring division and strife.

I still remember it. The year was 2000. I was in Birmingham, Alabama, for a large meeting. I stood speaking

> *Like the rock that was smitten, we too need to be broken, before the rivers of blessing can flow out through us to others. The opposition of men and their false accusations serve to keep us broken before God.*
>
> *—Zac Poonen*

to an acquaintance of mine and the whisperer used someone I barely knew to walk up and hurl a false accusation at me. I responded graciously realizing that he had been fed some erroneous information. To this day, however, the man will hardly get near me no matter how many times I've reached out to him. Whisperers sever fragile bonds of friendship and respect.

My simple example pales in comparison to another that I read. It bears a startling resemblance to Joseph's encounter. In his book *Hedges,* Jerry B. Jenkins gives practical advice for maintaining purity in a polluted world. Jenkins tells the true story of a young man who was an effective speaker and a great soulwinner, but very naïve. At a particular crusade, a beautiful young lady asked if she could meet with him privately. He tried to point her to one of the counselors, but she persisted. An hour or so later, the crowds dissipated and they were left alone. A few minutes later she fled the room screaming, "He made a pass at me! He wanted to make love to me!" The pastor in charge of the meeting went to the young man and demanded to know what happened when he was alone with the girl. The young man refrained from saying, but asked to face his accuser. The pastor agreed, but the crusade was cancelled.

Two nights later, the young lady with her parents met at the church with the pastor and the young man. The pastor asked if the young lady would like to say what happened. Her father replied that she had said all she was going to say. The pastor asked the young minister if he would like to tell what happened that night, but he refused saying, "I see no future in that. Only she and I know the truth, and I cannot defend myself."

The young minister then addressed the young lady. "You know what happened and what didn't happen in that room. If you don't tell the truth, I will be branded and may never preach again. This will damage my reputation and that of this church, and even that of God. If I did what you say I did, I deserve no better, but we both know that is not the truth."

The young lady finally admitted that she had told a lie. She had made a pass at the young minister but when he turned her down, she was embarrassed, ashamed, and angry. She lashed out at him with that story.

The whisperer is still at work in our world. Modern technology takes whispering to a new level. I remember spending summers with my grandparents at their lake house in rural East Texas. The lakeside residents had a party line, meaning that anyone around the lake could pick up the phone receiver and listen to whatever conversation was taking place. Where gossip once was done over the backyard fence or over the lunchroom counter, now it has moved light years ahead with

> *The effects of slander are always long-lived. Once lies about you have been circulated, it is extremely difficult to clear your name. It's a lot like trying to recover dandelion seeds after they have been thrown to the wind.*
>
> *—John MacArthur*

the advent of social media. Insults, insinuations, and innuendos are peddled amongst "friends" at warp speed. Whispering twenty-first-century style may seem modern and technologically advanced, but it is as old as the Garden.

We expect whispering in the world; we don't expect it in the church. One of the most hurtful experiences for believers is when those who should love them and uplift them choose to talk about them instead. Within churches, certain people can grow toxic: they always have the latest dirt and they're always spreading it. If a critical mass of such people is reached in a church, the entire congregation can grow toxic. Toxic churches will eventually run out of other people to talk about and will turn on one another. "If ye bite and devour one another," Paul warned, "take heed that ye be not consumed one of another" (Galatians 5:15).

Let me mention a few closing thoughts here. First, refrain from whispering. David once said all that hated him whispered about him (Psalm 41:7). When we whisper we reveal our hatred. Second, our inward life determines our speech. For good or evil, when we speak we reveal the contents of our heart (Luke 6:45). Think on those things that are pure, lovely, and of good report (Philippians 4:8). Finally, join forces with the encouragers—those people, like Barnabas of old, who seek the good in every situation. It takes no great genius to discover what's wrong with a person, but it takes spiritual insight to see diamonds in the rough and to focus on these.

Muzzle the whispering; unleash the encouraging!

CHAPTER 14:

UNTIL IRON ENTERS OUR SOULS

The whisperer achieves his momentary success when he blinds hearers to the truth and binds the righteous with a lie. Potiphar and perhaps his entire household believed the lie and Joseph was thrown into prison. Unjust accusations have the immediate impact of detouring, but they cannot derail God's immediate plans for a person's life.

Hell may have partied when Joseph was thrown down to prison. When the righteous person is cast down, the enemy should refrain from rejoicing (Micah 7:8, Proverbs 24:16). Joseph of Arimathea's borrowed tomb stands as proof positive to this lesson; so does Joseph's prison cell in Egypt. The same God whose voice transformed chaotic darkness to create this present world still speaks to turn a demonic detour into a divine destiny.

God told Jeremiah to take a trip to the potter's house. The prophet noticed the potter was able to modify marred lumps of clay into vessels of his pleasing. He made them over again. Through this potter, Jeremiah gained an insight into our redemptive God who doesn't give up easily, but continues to work on and work with a person to achieve His will (Jeremiah 18).

The enemy may have achieved his immediate aims, but these would prove to be short-lived. God used Joseph's trip to prison to accomplish a purpose. Whatever freedom and mobility Joseph possessed as a slave in Potiphar's house was taken from him. Joseph had been bound by the steep sides of a pit in Dothan, bound by the bonds that carried him into Egyptian slavery and now bound by prison. What was the point of this low point? God needed to put iron in Joseph's soul.

Psalms 105 says that God was behind the famine that soon came to Egypt and Canaan. Before the famine, however, he sent Joseph "who was sold for a servant: whose feet they hurt with fetters: he was laid in iron: until the time that his word came: the word of the LORD tried him" (Psalm 105:17-19). Besides being a single, strange sentence with the curious use of four colons, the psalmist captured the majesty and mystery of God's sovereignty.

Iron was not just put on him; it was placed in him. *Young's Literal Translation* says that Joseph's affliction had this result: "Iron hath entered his soul..." (Psalm 105:18, YLT). To the casual and carnal observer, Joseph was merely bound in iron; but to the spiritual observer, iron was entering into Joseph's soul. God uses the anvil of false accusations to form iron within our souls.

God prepares those He promotes. Over time the rose-colored glasses and naïve notions of this world are steadily removed. God uses time and circumstances to restrict the vistas of unlimited opportunities. We find ourselves in the blind canyons of few, if any, choices. In the valley He may restore our soul; but in prison He equips our soul with iron.

At the close of Moses' life, he blessed each of the tribes of Israel. Iron made its way into the blessing of the tribe of Asher. Moses prayed that Asher's foot would be dipped in oil, but the prayer didn't stop there. "Thy shoes shall be iron and brass; and as thy days, so shall thy strength be" (Deuteronomy 33:24-25). When the going gets rough,

God lashes our feet with shoes of iron and brass. For tough days, God provides tougher strength. Our trials serve to put iron in our souls.

The apostle of love, John, prayed that Gaius would prosper in all things as his soul prospered (III John 1:2). God seeks a balance between our inner world and outer world. Outward prosperity can be a curse if not preceded by inward prosperity. As God enlarges our influence and expands our reach, we must possess deeper stakes and longer cords (Isaiah 54:1-5). Tall buildings have deep foundations. To reach the heavens and to soar beyond our present limitations, we must possess deep, abiding, immovable principles and convictions. God's apt advice to those who would grow tall: "Dwell deep..." (Jeremiah 49:8).

> *Fame is a vapor, popularity an accident, riches take wing, and only character endures.*
>
> —*Horace Greeley*

What puts iron in our souls? Testing. The flesh sours in lean times, but the soul soars.

Joseph may not have attended the greatest schools of Egypt, but he was now enrolled in that Ivy League school known only to those who will be tested, tried, and approved of God: the University of Adversity. As an eagle soars on heated pockets of air known as thermals, the soul of man rises to its potential when the furnace of affliction is heated sevenfold.

"Times of great calamity and confusion have been productive for the greatest minds," said the oft-quoted nineteenth century cleric, Charles Caleb Colton. "The purest ore is produced from the hottest furnace. The brightest thunderbolt is elicited from the darkest storm."

One doesn't find diamonds in a rose garden; these are found in the deep places where pressure and heat have been applied.

The prosperity God planned for Joseph was great; thus, God sent him great adversity. Without affliction, we drift from God's plans for our lives; with affliction, we find the path He designed for us (Psalm 119:67). To be a weapon in God's hand against the famine to come, Joseph needed iron in his soul. He had to be afflicted.

The ancient Japanese craftsmen created the best swords in the known world. The sword maker's objective was to make the steel hard enough to retain a sharp edge, but soft enough to not be brittle and break in the time of testing. After much trial and error, the solution was found: a sword had to be made of both hard and soft steel. Multiple sheets of varying tensile strength of steel were heated, folded, and hammered together over and over again. A lengthy forging process rendered a sword formed with thousands of gossamer-thin layers of hard and soft steel. The end result is a weapon that will not break in the warrior's hand on the battlefield.

God is not only the Potter who makes vessels for daily use; He is also the Blacksmith who sharpens swords for battle. God seeks men and women of honor who are strong enough to withstand breaking in the tough times. The hard steel within our lives is God's Word and His unchanging character; the soft steel is our humility and dependence upon Him. Such steel is not forged in the high points, but is only formed in the low points.

God used prison to put iron in Joseph's soul. Joseph was not just marking time or experiencing yet another setback in his destiny; God was using this prison stint to prepare him for the day ahead. God was transforming Joseph into an extraordinary weapon in His mighty hands.

Remember this: present difficulty brings future glory (Romans 8:18). Each day of adversity brings you closer to graduation day. Each affliction overcome, each testing passed, each trial endured brings you closer to the day when God will reveal His glory in you. Just don't faint when the going gets rough.

Pain turns into gain; tragedy becomes triumph; and hurt turns to hope...if you don't faint. Fainting means your "strength is small" (Proverbs 24:10). So hold on and continue in what God has called you to do.

"Bless you, prison," said Russian dissident Alexander Solzhenitsyn, "for having been in my life." In the short-term we may not embrace our enrollment

> God never allows pain without a purpose in the lives of His children. He never allows Satan, nor circumstances, nor any ill-intending person to afflict us unless He uses that affliction for our good. God never wastes pain.
>
> —Jerry Bridges

in the University of Adversity, but over time we will recognize that success in life is defined less by the high points and more the low points. To not experience the forge of testing renders us less than useful for God's kingdom.

In the larger sense, God's purpose in permitting the unjust accusations and the adversity that followed was to put iron in Joseph's soul. In a practical sense, Joseph provides us with some lessons on how to appropriately handle unjust accusations. His behavior during this time permitted the hand of God to remain active in his life and to forge within his spirit and character the needed strength for the days ahead.

Truth hurts, but lies can hurt more. They always surprise us too. Joseph was going about his business as normal when he was genuinely accosted and then falsely accused. Recognizing that fiery darts come when we least expect them, we must always have the shield of faith in place. How does this shield reveal itself in Joseph's life? There are several practical ways.

First, we must recognize that people will say hurtful things. The tongue is the least controlled member of the body and can be "set on fire of hell" (James 3:6). Since Satan is the accuser, it's no surprise that he seeks to use man's tongue. When Simon Peter rebuked Jesus for mentioning His impending crucifixion, Jesus returned the rebuke by saying, "Get thee behind me, Satan" (Matthew 16:22-23). Peter had lent his voice to be used by the enemy. Fallen man will say hurtful things. As a corollary, it's generally true that hurting people hurt people.

In this same vein, it also follows that the accusations hurled by people reveal more about themselves than they do about their intended target. Jesus said that the words we speak "are spirit" (John 6:63), not speaking of the Holy Spirit but of our human spirit. Our speech is a tangible expression of our spirit. For this reason, Jesus said that it's not what goes into our mouth that defiles us, but what comes out of our mouth (Matthew 15:11). Our speech reveals that which we are and can defile what good remains in us.

Not only do people say hurtful things, the second practical lesson we learn is that we need not respond to false accusations. Over time, we grow to understand

> *No soul of high estate can take pleasure in slander. It betrays a weakness.*
>
> *—Blaise Pascal*

that people will say what they want to say and believe what they choose to believe. What is within our control is our response to unjust accusations. Someone said that each person brings two bottles into a conflict. One bottle is filled with gasoline that can be poured on the conflict to add to the fire; one bottle is filled with water that can extinguish the fire. Always choose water.

Call it the "Paradox of Proverbs." Solomon said in one verse to not answer a fool lest you be like him; in the next verse he says to answer a fool lest he be wise in his own eyes (Proverbs 26:4-5). Perhaps another way of saying this is that in the face of unjust accusations there are times when silence is golden and then there are times when silence is just plain yellow. Discretion is at times the better part of valor, but there are other times when we cannot keep silent in the face of the slanderer. We shouldn't keep silent when the accused is someone other than us, and we know that the accusation is false. Speaking up for others is expected and required of us. We should ordinarily refrain from speaking when we are the accused party unless it's a simple misunderstanding that can be easily corrected with some basic information. Rare is the moment when a person is afforded the opportunity to "set the record straight," and if that moment does appear, we should be cautious in using it.

Why? The more we speak, the guiltier we seem to people. In Shakespeare's *Hamlet*, Queen Gertrude says, "The lady doth protest too much, methinks." It's a quirk of fallen human nature: the more passionately we insist that something is false, the more people suspect the opposite is true.

The third practical lesson is that our lives should speak for themselves. I suspect there were many people in Potiphar's household who suspicioned that what his wife said was not true. They had observed Joseph and saw his scrupulous attention to detail, his fairness to others, and his manner of treating members of the opposite sex. Had Joseph carried on flirtatious and flagrant affairs with other members of the household, the accusations would have had greater credibility in the minds of those who knew Joseph the best.

"From henceforth let no man trouble me," the apostle Paul said at the close of his letter to the Galatians, "for I bear in my body the marks of the Lord Jesus" (Galatians 6:17). The scars on his body stood as mute sentinels and silent witnesses to what the apostle had suffered for the Lord's sake. People who have been tried, tested and healed of their hurts stand tall when others run.

Finally, we must at some point trust the Lord to be the righteous judge who sifts the false from the true. "We make a mistake in trying always to clear ourselves," observed Baptist preacher F. B. Meyer. "We should be wiser to go straight on, humbly doing the next thing, and leaving God to vindicate us. There may come hours in our lives when we shall be misunderstood, slandered, and falsely accused. But the believer takes his case into a higher court and lays it before his God."

The only way the accuser wins is if we let go of our integrity and divine destiny. Joseph refused to do this. He moved into the next station of his life, even though he had been wrongly accused and convicted. He didn't nurse grudges or dwell on the past. He was confident that a higher Power was at work in his life and that God would, in His own time and way, make things right.

Joseph would one day be made second in the nation of Egypt, meaning that Potiphar would answer to Joseph. Joseph secured the food for the entire nation as well, meaning that the survival of Potiphar and his wife depended upon his benevolence. When Joseph assumed this position, there is no record of him misusing or abusing his authority to go back and make the lives of his former employers miserable. Vindication is not God's primary purpose in our lives;

glory is. God will bring us through the low points that He may receive the glory.

In the rough places, look for iron to be put into your soul. God has more in store for you than a life of contentment. He is fashioning you to be of lasting value to His eternal Kingdom.

For a special video from the author with additional information, please visit the following:

http://thepointoflowpoints.wordaflamepress.com/lpsection5

DISCUSSION QUESTIONS

SECTION V: Combating Unjust Accusations

Chapters 13-14

Discuss the following questions:

1. What motivations do you think prompt a person to make a false accusation against another person?

2. Using Joseph as an example, how should a believer respond to unjust accusations?

3. Discuss the validity of this statement: unjust accusations say more about the accuser than the accused.

4. Discuss any instance in your personal life where an unjust accusation resulted in the accused not only being vindicated, but advancing past the accuser.

5. Joseph's patience in the arena of unjust accusations permitted iron to enter into his soul. Why is a person made stronger when he responds correctly to unjust accusations?

SECTION VI

JOSEPH'S FIFTH LOW POINT: REVIVING DYING DREAMS

CHAPTER 15:

HOSPITAL FOR BROKEN DREAMS

It had been a good try, but Joseph's efforts seemed to have fallen short. He had fallen from great heights at home and had worked himself up from the lowest ranks in Potiphar's house. Steadily, systematically, he had risen from the lowest station to the highest station until his world once again came crashing in. An unjust accusation put him back in bonds. It was as if the years spent in Egypt had not mattered at all.

> *Blessings alone do not open our eyes. Indeed, blessings by themselves tend to close our eyes. We do not come to know Him in the blessing, but in the breaking.*
>
> *—Chip Brogden*

We excuse quitters all the time, those people who for one reason or another just run into a string of bad decisions and worse outcomes and finally say, "I've had it!" Something deep within us relates to the down-and-outer who admits to himself and to others that he has no more to give and nothing to hope for and who only hopes for some quiet, peaceful corner to while out his days. Yes, the humane side of us would have understood if Joseph's story had ended here.

Had it ended there, however, we would probably have never known Joseph's story. For God sent Joseph to Egypt on a mission: save Egypt, save Canaan, save your family, and save the world. If Joseph had not succeeded, his brother Judah may have perished. Where would the future Lion of the Tribe of Judah be then? Israel was not yet a nation when Joseph was in Egypt, just a large family. When Israel and his family came to Egypt they numbered only seventy souls. The promises to Abraham, Isaac, and Jacob rested on a young man in his twenties who had been tossed into prison. He didn't seem to have much of a chance, nor did Israel.

Except God's hand remained on Joseph. The spotlight of human attention had left Joseph's face, but he was ever before God. The dream would live. But, like many other God-given hopes and promises, Joseph's dream would first fall deep into the ground and die before it could be born again.

Remember this name: Zaphnath-Paaneah. At the close of this final significant low point in Joseph's life, you will understand why God's people go through such times. Don't forget it! Zaphnath-Paaneah.

Joseph's losses were great. Early on he lost his mother. Shechem marks the place he lost his direction. He lost the affection of his brethren in Dothan. He lost his position in Potiphar's house. Through each loss God repositioned Joseph to be where He needed him to be. Joseph had excelled in Egypt, but he was in the wrong house. His ladder was leaning against the wrong building and no matter how high he climbed, he would not have reached God's intended destination. God did not need Joseph in the house of Pharaoh's captain of the guard, but in Pharaoh's house. Setbacks are God's preferred method to reposition us for greater glory. Low points cause us to change ladders where we might climb higher.

In this prison, Joseph would come in contact with two people from Pharaoh's house: the cupbearer or chief butler, and the chief baker. The first of these did more than serve Pharoah; he also served God's purpose in connecting Pharaoh and Joseph. Dreams formed the rungs on the ladder that led to Joseph's ascension into Pharaoh's house.

Dreams come to all. Within the soul of man is the ability to dream of a better world, a brighter future, a new you. God gives songs in the night. He gives visions of a new day and a brighter tomorrow.

In Bruce Wilkinson's allegorical tale, *The Dream Giver*, we read of a young man named Ordinary, a Nobody who lived in the land of Familiar. His world was about to change when he received an invitation to leave his Comfort Zone and to pursue his Big Dream. The invitation was punctuated by the arrival of a long, white feather.

Ordinary told his father about it. His father shared something with Ordinary that he had never heard. When his father had been a young man he too had received such an invitation. It came sealed as well with the feather. Fear kept him from leaving the land of Familiar. He chose to remain a Nobody and the long, white feather turned to dust.

Seeing the look on his father's face, Ordinary determined to not let that happen to him. He left the land of Familiar and went in pursuit of his big dream. Years later when his battles were won, Ordinary took the long, white feather, dipped it into ink and wrote to his father saying, "I discovered that every Nobody has a Dream, and it's never too late to pursue it."

Years before Joseph was tossed unceremoniously into prison, he too had dreamed. When the young boy shared his dreams with his father, they struck a cord in Jacob's heart. Jacob had dreamed too. Atop Bethel, Jacob dreamed of a golden ladder with angels ascending and descending upon it (Genesis 28). Upon returning to Canaan, Jacob had encountered the angelic host at Mahanaim (Genesis 32).

Jacob saw in his son Joseph a fellow dreamer.

Everyone dreams. It's a Spirit-inspired and anointed work to dream. The Holy Spirit moves on the old and young, male and female to see a different vision for this world and for our lives (Joel 2:28, Acts 2:17). The birth of Christ was accompanied by many dreams and visions. Joseph dreamed. Shepherds had an angelic vision. Simeon and Anna in the Temple were told by the Spirit they would see the Christ child (Luke 2). As the curtains of this age draw to a close in anticipation of Christ's return, we should expect more dreams, more visitations, and more prophetic words.

> *The appeal to God's sovereignty is not to foster hope that we will be spared all difficulty, but to foster confidence that when those difficulties come we are not abandoned. Things have not fallen out of hand. We can still rely on the God who has permitted us to face these things to supply us with the grace and help we need to be faithful under such circumstances.*
>
> *—D.A. Carson*

The Divine Designer is at work in our lives. He designs seemingly chance encounters, odd rendezvous, and serendipitous moments that usher in the dream. He opens doors; He shuts them. He sets the stage; He empties the stage. He turns the limelight of His favor upon us and then the clouds shroud the light. Obstacles, detours, and tedium are all tools of His trade. He knows what He's doing. This

Divine Designer of eternal dreams is sovereign and uses all things to prepare us for the larger stage before us.

Man is born to struggle; but man is also born to dream. In two chapters in I Kings, we see Solomon as struggler and Solomon as dreamer.

In I Kings 2, Solomon faced four adversaries: Joab, his cousin and would-be kingmaker; Shimei, Saul's descendant; Adonijah, his brother and rival; and Abiathar, the priest who fought his ascension to the throne of David. By the chapter's end, Benaiah—a faithful follower of David and Solomon—slew Adonijah, Joab, and Shimei. Abiathar received a fate worse than death; his banishment marked the end of the house of Eli's priesthood, something that had been prophesied years before in Shiloh (I Kings 2:27). Great dreams are born through great struggles.

In I Kings 3, the dream is born. Solomon went to Gibeon where the tabernacle of Moses then rested, minus the Ark that remained in David's tabernacle in Jerusalem. At Gibeon, Solomon offered one thousand sacrifices to God in thanks for seeing him through the struggles. God came to Solomon in a dream and asked, "What do you want me to give to you?" (I Kings 3:5). Solomon asked for wisdom, but in his dream God gave him this and so much more: prosperity, honor, and longevity (3:13-14). When Solomon awoke, he realized God had come to him in a dream. He hastened to Jerusalem and there he worshiped before the Ark of the Covenant.

"If there were dreams to sell," posed the Romanticist poet Thomas Lovell, "what would you buy?" Every dream has a price tag. The currency for purchasing dreams is not coinage, but carnage. Solomon's dream required sacrifice. The dream of the church cost Jesus His own blood (Acts 20:28). All things magnificent emerge from full devotion.

Dreamers of great dreams share many qualities with Joseph.
Dreamers:

- Have a firm conviction that God is at work in their lives. Joseph inasmuch told Pharaoh this in their first meeting. He told Pharaoh that the ability to interpret dreams come from God (Genesis 41:15-16).
- Don't cling to the past, but look instead to the future. Joseph readily forgave his brethren.
- See opportunity. Joseph found opportunity in Potiphar's house. He also excelled in prison.
- Stay focused on solutions. Joseph didn't curse the darkness; he learned to strike a match. When faced with the fearsome enemy of a famine, Joseph was prepared with a solution.
- Give of themselves. Joseph held nothing back in his service.
- Refuse to give up. Life is like wrestling a gorilla. You don't quit when you're tired; you quit when the gorilla gets tired. Joseph was like the "man in the arena" described by the late President Theodore Roosevelt, "whose face is marred by dust and sweat and blood; who strives valiantly...." Joseph was that man. Most dreamers are as well.
- Exercise personal responsibility. Joseph could have blamed anyone and everyone for his predicament, but he chose to realize the steering wheel was in his hands and with it he could steer clear of the foxholes of self-pity and victimization.

Riding alongside great dreams are great attitudes. People who possess both are apt to see their dreams come true. No one said, however, it would be easy.

Dreams too often become junkyard relics. What was once valued no longer has the wheels or will to go forward and is trashed with the menagerie of "couldas," "wouldas," and "shouldas." Dreams can flatline, never to be resuscitated back to life.

In a series taught by Mike Connell, he identifies three "dream-killers" or "dream thieves." The first is undeveloped character. If we dream of having a new car or a new house, then character may not be the fundamental issue. Yet, suspended above Joseph were promises of ruling and reigning. It takes time to form character fit for a king. Without character, dreams are short-lived. The second and third "dream thieves" are delays and disappointments. Deep valleys of postponement and discouragement protect lofty dreams.

Years ago, Barbara Johnson penned her autobiographical work, *Where Does a Mother Go to Resign?* Sometimes, when I think I have troubles, I go back and read this book again and my troubles dissipate. Her husband was in a near-fatal car accident and suffered debilitating injuries from this. She lost one son in Vietnam and another fell victim to a drunk driver. Her youngest son then confessed he was a homosexual and separated himself from her. She formed Spatula Ministries, for peeling people off of the ceiling and putting them back on the road to recovery. She faced the low points and chose to pick flowers, not weeds. "We can face the inevitable," wrote Johnson, "and realize that we have greater reserves and resources than we thought possible."

Where does a dreamer go to resign? You've been there. Once you ran through grassy fields bathed in warm sunshine intoxicated by the beauty and majesty of your dream, but now you're laboring under dark, heavy skies and you feel that life has forgotten you. Raindrops mingle with tears and your mind plays tricks on you. You wonder if this is a dream or a wish.

Don't think it strange when this happens. It's happened before and I'm sure it will happen many more times. Dreams must be brought low, before the dreamer can be taken high. We have to be willing to place every Isaac on the altar. Only then can the dream be fully realized.

Dreams may get sick, but dreams don't die easily. Thus, dreamers can't afford to give up. When the dream seems to be on life-support, that's when we must determine how serious we are about seeing the dream come to life.

- Abraham was serious about his dream. He fought the vultures away from his covenantal sacrifice (Genesis 15).
- Rizpah clung to the tiniest thread of a dream before her five sons' prone figures. She too fought away the fowls by day and the beasts by night (II Samuel 21).
- Job faced the loss and destruction of everything, but he shouted "I know my Redeemer lives!" (Job 19:25).

The thief comes to steal and kill one's dreams if it's possible. To be theft-proof, a dream must be wrapped up and consecrated in prayer, passion, and purpose. The dream must work is way deep into the warp and woof of a person's spirit. It must be impervious to criticism, doubt and persecution. If knowledge is power; certainty is more powerful. When it comes to a dream, certainty almost reigns supreme. Wistfulness melts like the morning dew, but a true dream can survive the lowest of low points.

Dreams are like seeds; they die only to be born again. Dreams are like herbs underfoot; crush them and their fragrance and seeds are released to bless the world. Dying and crushed dreams can be resuscitated.

While surfing online recently through some news sites, I happened upon an unusual hospital. I live in Houston, home to the Texas Medical Center that features world-class hospitals devoted to many varied specialties. Yet I'd never heard of the hospital that I read about in Naples, Italy. Two hundred years ago, a stage manager named Luigi worked for a local opera. In the course of his work he repaired and repainted a few of the puppets used onstage. He left these repaired puppets outside his door for them to cure and dry. Passersby noticed the puppets and asked Luigi if he could repair keepsakes and treasures from their childhood along with precious heirlooms handed down through the generations. Each had been broken; each needed repaired. One of these early Napolitano visitors christened Luigi's repair shop, the "Doll Hospital."

Luigi's descendants would continue the work. To this day, the hospital is filled with antique dolls missing eyes, limbs, or other features. Owners of these masterpieces from days gone by seek restoration.

"I repair objects of love," said the present proprietor. "People come here to have their broken dreams restored."

God's House is the Hospital for Broken Dreams. I think of Mephibosheth, Jonathan's son and Saul's grandson. When the fateful news came from Mount Gilboa of Jonathan's and Saul's deaths, Mephibosheth was a small child. His nurse picked him up and raced from the palace in an effort to save the child's life. In her haste, she dropped the child and he became lame on both feet (II Samuel 9:3). His existence became pitiful and miserable. He dwelt in the backwater town of Lo-Debar. His life became a rhythmic, dull poem: Born to the house of Saul, injured in the house of fall, and embittered in the house of gall. Broken dreams indeed...A prince had become a pauper.

There are many Mephibosheths around us. We live in the land of broken people. Think of the lines from the nursery rhymes and songs we learned as a child: Humpty Dumpty had a great fall; London Bridge is falling down; Jack fell down and broke his crown; and three blind mice. Early on, we were clearly taught we live in a broken world filled with broken people.

Sunset Boulevard in Los Angeles, California, has been called the boulevard of broken dreams. The once bright-eyed youth who came to the West Coast to live the dream are now rendered dull and broken on this street. In a watercolor of the same title painted by Gottfriend Helnwein, the images of Humphrey Bogart, Marilyn Monroe, and James Dean are depicted seated at a diner counter. The waiter behind the counter is Elvis Presley. Like these late celebrities, many others have followed the setting sun of momentary visions only to end up walking that same boulevard of broken dreams.

King David ran a hospital for broken dreams. His mighty men had recovered their dreams in his presence, but David did not stop there—he reached not just for the mighty, but also for the broken. David invited Saul's broken grandson to live in his palace and to eat at his table. David made Mephibosheth welcome in his home. A prince was restored to the palace.

Do you remember when the Son of David cleansed God's house? He drove out the self-satisfied and made room for the hurting and wounded. In Matthew's Gospel we read that once the Temple had been cleansed, the blind and lame came to Jesus in the Temple and they were healed (Matthew 21:14). If we make room for the broken dreams in our midst, they can be made whole.

In a sense, Joseph ran a hospital for broken dreams in the prison. He could not do much about his own lot, but he could help other dreamers. Joseph extended his hands to others, and God would one day extend His scepter to Joseph and his dreams would be restored.

CHAPTER 16:

AN EGYPTIAN RESURRECTION

If God wanted to alter our direction, how would He do it? Would He rent a billboard alongside the road of life which says, "Hey, turn here!"? Would He send an armed motorcade, a scrawled message on sepia-toned paper in a floating bottle or a text from cyberspace? God communicates through His Word, His Spirit and through His faithful ministers. He generally whispers; He rarely shouts.

If His message failed to get through, however, He may allow the enemy to stage what could be called a "reversal of fortune." God permits low points to enter our lives through which we change our perspective, our purpose and our plans. More times than not, when the stakes are immense, God speaks to us in life's low points.

Joseph changed tracks in this fifth and final low point recorded in his life. The first mention of a prison in the King James Version of the Bible is in Joseph's fifth low point. "Joseph's master took him, and put him into the prison..." (Genesis 39:20). The Hebrew word for prison (*cohar*) can also be translated as fortress, tower, or a roundhouse.

Roundhouse...

Nearly two centuries ago, a different sort of roundhouse was first built in England. The roundhouse had numerous entrances through which steam locomotives could enter. Within the roundhouse was a section of track on a turntable that could pivot the steam engine. The engine could then exit in a different direction than what it had entered, it could even be turned a complete 180 degrees and exit pointing in the opposite direction it had entered.

What engineers did for trains, the Creator does for people. He recalibrates, repositions, and realigns our lives to bring the most glory to His name. Since the wise men encountered the baby Jesus in Bethlehem and left a different way, people through the centuries have come in one way, but left a different way.

Joseph was in Egypt where God wanted him, but he was slightly off track. His roundhouse experience served to alter the trajectory of Joseph's life and to lead the train of divine redemption to its intended destination. For the prison where Joseph was placed was not just any prison, it was reserved for the "king's prisoners" (Genesis 39:20). Through this prison, God made a slight change to Joseph's trajectory and in so doing, Joseph saw his dreams fulfilled. In a similar way, when we walk through a low point, God repositions our lives.

Soon, what Joseph had been to Potiphar he became to the prison keeper. He ascended to the place where he was in charge of the prison—a prisoner supervising the imprisoned. Time passed and with it a young man matured. His leadership and administrative abilities were finely honed. People in authority trusted him; people in his care looked up to him. Imperceptibly and incrementally, Joseph moved to the place God needed him.

It's not an exaggeration to say that dreams put Joseph in prison. Dreams separated him from his brethren and provoked their jealousy in Dothan. His desire to see these dreams fulfilled caused him to reject the advances of Potiphar's wife. Dreams had brought him to this roundhouse and dreams would bring him out.

One day two of the new royal inmates dreamed. They came to Joseph asking if he could interpret their dreams. The ability to dream comes to all, but only to a select few comes the insight and foresight to interpret a dream. Joseph knew dreams as few could. He was like the counterfeit detector who could detect the fake because he had handled the real thing so much. Joseph could sense, feel, and anticipate what God was saying in a person's dream. He understood his own dream; now, God directed him to make known the dreams of others.

He listened patiently to the dreams of the two men. The interpretation of each dream that came to Joseph was different. He sensed the chief butler would receive honor and be elevated to his original position, but the chief baker would receive horror and be executed. Joseph was confident enough in his interpretations to convey the same to these two men saying that they would both happen in three days.

Joseph implored the chief butler to not forget him when he was elevated to Pharaoh's household. He summarized his entire life in a single sentence. "I was stolen away out of the land of the Hebrews," Joseph told the chief butler, "and here also have I done nothing that they should put me into the dungeon" (Genesis 40:15). Consider this single sentence. No self-pity, blame shifting, or finger pointing can be found, only a matter-of-fact statement of what had been his life to this point.

Shortly thereafter, Pharaoh decided the fates of these two men as Joseph had indicated. Days passed. Months passed. No word came from Pharaoh's household. Scripture puts the epitaph on this chapter with these words: "Yet did not the chief butler remember Joseph, but forgat him" (Genesis 40:23). Joseph was forgotten.

Joseph saw another's dream fulfilled, but not his own. He was amongst the forgotten dwelling in the shadows of obscurity. Others achieved, but his hopes and visions were placed on hold.

As I mentioned in the interlude about Hurricane Ike, the winds of the storm followed by months of inattention brought great damage to our church. The recognition had come that we were in for the fight of our lives—trying to help the church survive while at the same time seeking ways to restore the facilities to their former condition. God awakened me early one morning and a word was ringing in my heart and mind. The word was "afterward."

Over the next few hours, I prayed about this word and searched the Scriptures until my attention rested on the second chapter of Joel. What begins with sounding alarms and prophetic days of gloom ends with stirring promises. God promised to restore the years that were taken from His people due to the plague sent amongst them. This is followed by that passage of Scripture

> *God does not need those who praise him when in a state of euphoria. He needs those who are in love with him when in distress....This is the task: in the darkest night to be certain of the dawn, certain of the power to turn a curse into a blessing, agony into a song. To know the monster's rage and, in spite of it, proclaim to its face (even a monster will be transfigured into an angel); to go through hell and to continue to trust in the goodness of God—this is the challenge and the way.*
>
> *—Abraham Heschel*

quoted on the day of Pentecost, "And it shall come to pass afterward, that I will pour out my spirit upon all flesh; and your sons and your daughters shall prophesy, your old men shall dream dreams, your young men shall see visions: and also upon the servants and upon the handmaids in those days will I pour out my spirit" (Joel 2:28-29).

"Afterward!" I whispered aloud to no one but myself. "It shall come to pass afterward!" The Lord seemed to be saying to me that there will always be an afterward. No matter how dismal and bleak the present, a new day will dawn. Irrespective of today's hurt and pain, healing will soon come.

Joel caught a glimpse of the mysterious ways of God—that on the heels of judgment and affliction come waves of mercy and affection. With those spiritual waves come fresh dreams, prophecies, and visions. Yesterday's dreams may seem to have vanished beneath the hurt and despair, but there shall always be an "Afterward!" Can you sense that? Can you sense that God is bidding you to cling to your dreams come what may? Within those dreams lie tomorrow's possibilities.

"Tell me your dreams," Yonggi Cho, pastor of the world's largest church, once said, "and I will prophesy your future." Today's dream is tomorrow's reality.

The greater the dream, the greater the likelihood it will be sent to the graveyard. Some dreams never make it back; others don't stay long.

In Romans 6:4, Paul said that we have been buried with Christ in baptism. In the next verse, he said that we have been planted in the likeness of his death. There is an implied difference in being buried and being planted. The undertaker buries and the farmer plants. The undertaker expects what he buries to remain buried, but the farmer expects what he planted to reappear.

God-given dreams may appear to be buried, but they are actually only planted. A divine purpose may disappear from sight for a while, but it will arise again. And when it comes back it will be increased thirty-, sixty- and a hundredfold. Joseph's dream was planted so he may multiply to fill the earth.

There may come times in your life that you will have to speak forcefully to your dream. Like the widow of Nain's son, a Code Blue will be called over your dream and it will lay dormant and seem beyond resurrection. Speak life into your dream. Like Ezekiel standing before a valley filled with very dry bones, you will sometimes be forced to speak to your broken dreams. Exhale a promise from God over the moribund dream and watch a resurrection take place.

Parents should learn to speak to their children's dreams. Speak a blessing and not a cursing. As the patriarchs of old, paint a picture of a coming day when God is going to fulfill the desires of their hearts. See and say what you sense God has planned for them. Someday they will remember it and perhaps they too will see a resurrection of their dreams.

Two things were noticed after the Great Fires of 1666 had passed over London, destroying much of the city. New instances of the Black Death that had wreaked havoc in London the prior year were not reported. The fire had destroyed the plague. The fire had also so thoroughly warmed the ground that seeds buried deep in the earth were germinated and began to grow. Forgotten species of plants and flowers emerged the following spring in London.

The crucible of affliction can produce similar results. The alloy of insincerity and lesser dreams are skimmed away while the rare treasure emerges. Soon, the prison walls holding Joseph would fall away. The false accusations would soon melt away. Joseph would walk away from the prison and be promoted to the place where God desired for him to be.

At the end of Genesis 40, the chief butler forgot Joseph. A new chapter, however, was about to start. Genesis 41 opens with Pharaoh experiencing twin troubling dreams. Egyptian wise men and magicians could not conjure up the meaning of their king's dreams. Then the chief butler remembered Joseph.

Word came to the prison: "Joseph! Pharaoh calls for Joseph!" When the word of release comes, it will happen authoritatively and decisively. The quibbling of the past few years will cease and a certain sound will reverberate through the steep walls of your deepest valley. It was God's time. God was prepared to do in Egypt what no one else could do. The King of kings would take an earthly king by the hand and move the heavens and earth to protect one of His children. God's time had come.

> "Afflictions add to the saints' glory. The more the diamond is cut, the more it sparkles; the heavier the saints' cross is, the heavier will be their crown."
>
> —Thomas Watson

A quick makeover took place. Joseph was transformed from a prisoner to a prince. He shaved stubble from his face. He bathed. He put on a change of clothing. Shackles were removed. A chin rose. Shoulders were pushed back. Joseph marched from obscurity into history.

Anyone can dream. Few can interpret. Fewer still can take an interpretation and map out a future so breathtaking that a king admits—God is in this! Joseph was in the rarefied atmosphere of those who could do all three: dream, interpret, and act on the dream. When his moment came, God made sure he was ready.

He went into the roundhouse of prison only to emerge from there on the right tracks. He was prepared. He waited on his time to come and come it did, in a moment—a twinkling of an eye. He was changed. He experienced an Egyptian resurrection.

God's plan marches forward though it may take a while to reveal itself. What the enemy means for evil, God works for good. God recycles defeat into victory; shame into success; midnight into morning; and limping into leaping.

Yet, what Joseph experienced was not really about him at all. He was God's chosen vessel to bless others and to cause Pharaoh to realize the almighty hand of God. Through Joseph's efforts, Egypt and Canaan were spared. Through Joseph, Pharaoh glorified the one true God.

Rachel had named her firstborn son, Joseph—"May God add more." Pharaoh gave Joseph a new name, Zaphnath-Paaneah. The most powerful man in the most powerful nation on earth called Joseph: "God still speaks; God still lives."

Have you ever thought about your low points in this manner? That what you're going through may not be about you at all. Your experiences in life may not be caused by what you did or didn't do, but by what God is seeking through your life and longing to show others. As you endure the low point, God is preparing you to be a greater blessing to someone else, thereby causing God to receive greater glory.

As surely as this globe is spinning on an invisible axis while hurtling through space, you're moving steadily toward what God has for you. Pray in the Spirit. Lift the shield of faith. Be prepared. Your day will come.

For a special video from the author with additional information, please visit the following:

http://thepointoflowpoints.wordaflamepress.com/lpsection6

CLOSING COMMENTS

In the fifty chapters of Genesis, one-fourth of the chapters focus on the life of Joseph. His story starts in Genesis 30 and carries forward to Genesis 50. The five low points in Joseph's life all took place prior to his thirtieth birthday. He lived another eighty years beyond this time and the nation of Israel flourished.

Another Pharaoh who "knew not Joseph" would arise and persecute Israel (Exodus 1:8). So began the persecution and trauma that led to the coming Exodus and return to the Promised Land that Abraham had foreseen many years before (Genesis 15:16).

Joseph died at the ripe age of 110 years. He lived long enough to bury his father. He got to see his grandchildren; great grandchildren; and great, great grandchildren. Before he died, Joseph told the children of Israel that God would visit them in the future. And he made them promised that his bones would not remain in Egypt. In the closing verse of Genesis, Joseph died, was embalmed and placed in a coffin awaiting his funeral procession (Genesis 50:26).

As instructed by Joseph, his family would take his bones out of Egypt. It seems that the task fell to Joshua, one of Ephraim's descendants (Joshua 24:32). The world's largest and longest funeral procession took place during the forty years from the Exodus to the conquest of Canaan's land. Joseph's remains were carried beneath a pillar of cloud by day and fire by night. Joseph's remains crossed over the Red Sea. Kept with the tribe of Ephraim west of the Tabernacle, Joseph's remains spent many years crossing the wilderness. Finally his coffin was carried across the Jordan River into the Promised Land.

Joseph was not buried outside of Bethlehem with his mother Rachel. He was not buried in Hebron with the patriarchs of Abraham, Isaac, and Jacob. Scripture does not say that Joseph named the place of his burial, but it's likely that Joshua was fulfilling his ancestor's request. Joseph was buried in Shechem, the place where he had met the supposed divine Stranger while wandering in the fields. He was buried in one of the low points of his life.

When you reach the end of your days, you will probably look back and sense that your low points were where you found God to be the most real and your life took on new meaning. Low points define, shape and make us who God wants us to be. That's the point of low points.

In a Harvard University study of 173 men that traced them from their graduation in the early 1940s through their adult lives, the simple truth emerged: how a person handles crisis determines his satisfaction with life. If he can handle life's blows without blame and bitterness, he will do well in life.

Joseph is called the "Jesus of the Old Testament." Egypt needed a savior; God sent her Joseph. You and I are sent as divine representatives to our generation. Our world needs to see Jesus afresh and anew. What is happening to you is less about you and more about Him—making Him visible to this present day world.

How you endure life's low points determines how God elevates you. If you can walk through life's dark valleys without losing your faith in God; if you can hold to His hand through prayer and meditation on the Word; if you can keep your heart free and clear of bitterness and strife; then, God will do through you what He did through Joseph—He will bless you and spare others.

May high praise come from your next low point! God is with you and is doing something wonderful in you.

DISCUSSION QUESTIONS

SECTION VI: Reviving Dying Dreams

Chapters 15-16 and closing comments

Discuss the following questions:

1. Pharaoh gave Joseph the name, Zaphnath-Paaneah: "God still speaks; God still lives." What in your opinion causes unbelievers to see Jesus in us?

2. The Harvard study cited in the closing chapter indicates that a person who can respond well to life's hardships will more than likely succeed at what they're doing. Discuss how important such a quality is in life.

3. Consider the author's statement in the book: "Your experiences in life may not be caused by what you did or didn't do, but by what God is seeking through your life and longing to show others." How have you found this to be true in your life?

4. As we draw to the close of this study, let's return to those envelopes we sealed at the first session. Please open your envelope. Take a moment to look at the low points you listed and think about why God may have permitted each of these to come to your life. Based on what we've learned in this study, would you please share one of these low points with the group and why you believe God permitted it to happen and how you've grown stronger because of it.